Feb. 1999
Round Table Book

CREATE A SAFER WORLD

IDEAS FOR REDUCING VIOLENCE IN YOUR COMMUNITY

Woman's Missionary Union
Birmingham, Alabama

Woman's Missionary Union
P. O. Box 830010
Birmingham, AL 35283-0010

Dewey Decimal Classification: 303.6
Subject Headings:
CHURCH AND SOCIAL PROBLEMS
HUMAN RELATIONS
VIOLENCE

Cover design by Tim Robinson

ISBN: 1-56309-251-4

W984105•0598•5M1

CONTENTS

Promote Peace in Families 1

Pursue Peace in Communities 11

Extend the Walls of the Church .22

Care for, Love, and Protect Children 29

Nurture and Equip Youth 36

Diminish the Lure of Gangs 45

Cultivate Domestic Harmony 57

Respect Your Elders 66

Build Bridges of Love 73

The Unspeakable Crime 80

Throw Down the Sticks and Stones 87

Put the Sport Back in Sports 97

Control the Television Controls 105

Diffuse Workplace Disagreements 115

Develop a Heart to Help the Poor 123

Promote Mental Wholeness 131

Lessen the Likelihood of Suicide 140

Work Within the Criminal Justice System 148

Resources for Further Help 156

Appendix A: Caring for the Caregiver 170

Appendix B: How to Develop a Care Team 172

Appendix C: Support Groups .175

Appendix D: Mentoring 177

Appendix E: Networking 179

Appendix F: Project Peacemaking Plan 181

Appendix G: Screening Volunteers 183

Appendix H: Teaching Plan 186

Appendix I: Project Literacy 189

Endnotes 191

PROMOTE PEACE IN FAMILIES

By Karen Dockrey

Is it really possible to create a safer world? Can we really curb the violence that plagues our communities, nation, and world? We can, but we won't unless we begin within our homes. Much of the violence that spills into our streets has its origins in the family.

> Young Jenna watches Mom and Dad argue. She goes to school sad and can't concentrate on her work. She gets a D on her spelling test. In frustration she lashes out at her best friend, saying ugly words she regrets for months.

> Larry, a newlywed, comes home from work exhausted. When his wife Lisa wants to talk, he yells at her to be quiet and leave him alone. When she says she just wants a minute, he slaps her and says, "I told you to be quiet!"

> Eli, a teenager, wonders why his mother abandoned the family. A kind boy who would never hurt anyone, his sadness grows into rage. He does poorly in school and is suspended. He meets other troubled boys, and together they begin to steal, taking purses from tourists. "All I'm taking is money; I don't hurt anybody," Eli reasons. When the trio joins a gang, Eli's reasoning moves one step further: "Here is a group that will never desert me. For them I'll steal even if people do get hurt."

1

How might both Jenna and her schoolmates be happier if Jenna's mother assured her before she left for school, "It's OK, honey. Dad and I are not permanently mad. We just misunderstood each other. We have it worked out now"?

How much more loving would Larry and Lisa's marriage be if Larry took a minute to hear Lisa before resting? What closeness would grow if Lisa talked briefly before letting Larry rest? What good would grow as each considered the other's needs as well as his or her own?

Why did Eli have to turn to a gang to find the togetherness he missed in his family? How much rage would have been saved if Eli's father had helped him through his grief? How might Eli have reached his potential as an engineer if a teacher had listened to Eli's anger, given him skills for doing his schoolwork, and believed in him while insisting on good behavior?

BIBLICAL FOUNDATIONS

Peace boils down to relationship skills. What actions, words, and attitudes can we use to bring joy into each other's lives? How can we help each other with problems rather than letting problems divide us? How can we understand sadness and anger, healing it rather than escalating it to violence? How can we care for each other in Jesus' name? As individual families and churches we can work toward peace. We can halt the tragedy of family-born violence. We can recognize that getting along with any other person is difficult. Then we can take deliberate action to make certain we not only get along but live in peace. The Bible says it like this:

> "Live in harmony with one another. Do not be proud, but be willing to associate with people of low position. Do not be conceited. Do not repay anyone evil for evil. Be careful to do what is right in the eyes of everybody. If it is possible, as far as it depends on you, live at peace with everyone. Do not be overcome by evil, but overcome evil with good" (Rom. 12:16–18,21).

Being a person of peace takes supernatural power. It's not easy to swallow pride and conceit to work for harmony and overcome evil. The natural response is to be selfish, to get revenge, to keep score. But as spiritual people, we can move past these natural impulses to:

•see the other person's point of view;
•stop the evil pattern rather than continue it;
•forgive and ask God to help us leave it behind.

We can act our way into a new way of feeling. While not all Christians acknowledge and accept it, God promises us the power to do this: "And my God will meet all your needs according to his glorious riches in Christ Jesus" (Phil. 4:19).

The peace needs God will meet include:

•ideas for knowing what to say and do in a potentially explosive situation;
•words that show understanding and ease confusion;
•actions that calm emotions;
•attitudes that bring peace;
•relationship skills that prevent hostility from developing;
•an understanding of how actions influence others, enabling us to choose actions that bring God's desired result;
•patterns that give family members a haven from the violence they face outside the family;
•motivation to keep on working for peace;
•recognition that peace and violence prevention are continuing patterns, not instant solutions.

Trust and obey your God. Because He lived on earth in the person Jesus Christ, He knows what it's like to live in a family. He knows just what to do when misunderstandings and other problems occur (Luke 2:48–52). Besides all that, He can see the present, future, and past. He can help you in just the right way. Let Him do so.

4
SEEKING SOLUTIONS

. . . Within the Home

Peace comes through purposeful caring. Because none of us is born knowing how to create peace, we all need practice. Let these ideas get you going:

•**Joy focus:** Decide to focus on bringing joy into each other's lives rather than aggravation. Joy is different than happiness and does not equal giving in. Sometimes joy producing means asking to share a chore or talking. In all cases it means taking the action that brings good to both sides.

•**Temper tags:** Find words or cues that warn of intense emotion in you or another family member. Use this as a humorous and nonthreatening way to alert the family. Let it prevent eruption of violent words or actions. For example, say, "I'm wearing red," to indicate anger. Imitate the emergency beeps on radio following by phrases like: "If this had been an actual temper, people would have been hurt. Stay tuned for further information." Or, "Warning: This girl is about to explode." Let these temper tags build communication, not take the place of it. The goal is to signal others so you can vent without inflaming.

•**Doorknob hangers:** Involve the family in designing individual doorknob hangers. One which says *Skies are blue* indicates that the family member is feeling cooperative. One which says *Partly cloudy* indicates that the family member is struggling, but not uncooperatively so. *Storm brewing* indicates a touchy mood that could explode. These signs don't give excuses for prickly behavior but indicate the weather conditions before conversation begins.

•**"How was your day?"** Each time you gather with any family member, ask about the events of his or her day. Then listen with rapt attention. Just knowing someone cares about the ups and downs of life gives family members resources to manage them.

•**Refuse all hate words:** Never allow a racial joke, an ugly comment, or words that declare one person below another. The way we talk about people influences how we treat them. Halting hate language can powerfully promote unity among people, even the people in your own family.

•**Know that getting along is hard:** Any time there's more than one person, conflicts, confusion, and catastrophes can follow. Don't use energy worrying about the fact that you have them; give your energy to solving them. Attack the conflicts rather than each other. Communicate until you clear up confusion. Face the catastrophes as a united team rather than letting your pain consume each other.

•**Leave guilt behind:** Too often we feel so badly about struggling to get along that we take no action at all. Refuse to let guilt incapacitate you. Instead learn new patterns to replace destructive ones, find forgiveness where needed, declare false guilt false, and then move on to do good. Let present good heal past hurt. When Satan continues to torment you, remind him that God has forgiven you and you're now focusing on doing right.

•**Learn the lingo:** Certain words and tones bring joy. The Bible says: "A gentle answer turns away wrath, but a harsh word stirs up anger" (Prov. 15:1). Deliberately stop explosive words to replace them with peace-building words. Here are some examples:

Violence-Causing	Peace-Building
"That was so stupid!"	"Everybody makes mistakes. What have you learned?"
"Get out of my face!"	"I need some privacy, please."
"Where do you get such ideas!"	"Unique idea! It just might work."
"Don't you have *any* feelings?"	"It really hurts when you do that."

"If he likes you, he must not know you."	"He sees the good in you."
"You'll never amount to anything."	"You can do whatever you set your mind to."
"You're one problem after another."	"We'll solve your problems together."
"Why do you keep your head in the clouds?"	"If you dream it, you can do it."

•**Lingo race:** Challenge family members to come up with five phrases a week that promote peace. Notice that some of the youngest family members are the best at this.

•**Problem focus:** Solve one problem at a time with a process that works for your family, attacking the problem rather than each other. Try the following method: (1) list all solutions, even silly ones; (2) choose one; (3) implement it; (4) evaluate it and change what needs changing; and (5) put it into practice.

•**Mad means sad:** When someone is angry, automatically ask, "What's bothering you?" Just hearing the circumstances defuses some rage. Defuse the rest together by finding ways to solve the problem. Never excuse selfish behavior based on anger; instead hear it long enough to find its solution. If your daughter is mad because she was cut from the team, decide on intense practice in preparation for the next tryouts, and find a way for her to participate at some level in the meantime.

•**Television talk:** Each time you watch a television show or witness a world event, talk about how well or how poorly the people involved practiced peace. Take turns asking, "How does God want us to imitate this or act differently?"

•**Clear but kind:** Learn to say exactly what you mean and feel in ways that are kind and caring. Kindness means stating all ideas, feeding them into God's harvester so He can produce the wheat and discard the chaff.

•**Kinder still:** Each day find a way to grow even kinder in tone and attitude. Ask, "How can I imitate Jesus Christ more completely and build unity based in Him? How can I really hear what my family member is saying?"

•**Peace pursuit:** Regularly find a new way to practice peace in your family. Resources include the Bible, Christian books, and the Baptist Peace Fellowship. As you search for peace passages in your Bible, discover ways to live them. "Out of the mouths of babes" on page 8 offers examples. These passages show that each person chooses or denies peace. It's not luck or blessing; it's simply choosing to obey God with actions and attitudes that bring His good. Peace isn't something you own; it's something you do. You can't fake it. You can't use the words without the actions. You genuinely, and with God's help, choose to express peace.

... Within the Church

Churches are made up of real people with real wisdom given by our real God. As we share our ideas and express our love, we equip all families to live peacefully. Here are 15 ideas:

•**Weekly print a "peace pattern":** Use the announcement section of your church newsletter to print one of the above ideas, closing with these lines: "Together we're learning how to live peacefully in our families. Please share with us a way your family practices peace. With your permission we'll print it with or without your name. Thanks for helping us all to grow in Christ."

•**Be teachable:** Destruction happens when church leaders present a "We know it all and we're out to fix your family" stance. No one Christian, no matter how wise, knows everything there is to know about families. Each family, no matter how great its struggle, has something to share with others. Work as a team.

•**Out of the mouths of babes:** Invite children in your church to teach about peace, writing their words for your church newsletter or to read during worship. Choose a different child each week, inviting him or her to explain how to live peacefully according to a Bible verse such as one of the following: 2 Kings 9:22; 2 Chronicles 14:5; Psalms 4:8; 37:11,37; Numbers 6:24–26; 1 Samuel 1:17; 20:42; Proverbs 12:20; 14:30; 16:7; 17:1; 29:17; Isaiah 9:6–7; Ezekiel 13:10–16; 37:26; Malachi 2:5–6; Luke 1:78–79; Romans 2:9–11; 5:1; 14:19; Galatians 5:22–23; 6:16; Ephesians 2:14; 4:3; Philippians 4:7; Colossians 1:20; 1 Thessalonaians 5:13; 2 Timothy 2:22; Hebrews 12:14; James 3:18.

•**Teach true theology:** Rather than saddle families with "If you really love Jesus, you'll find it easy to live peacefully," assure families that getting along with any other person is difficult. Passages like Romans 7:15 and 8:3 show that each time we allow God to help us, we can move past the difficulties to the good on the other side.

•**Encourage deliberate action:** There's a dangerous myth going around that if you have to think about it, love is not love. Purposeful peacemaking is no less valuable than spontaneous peace. God had a plan when He created the earth; He blesses our plans to love family members.

•**Pronounce pride poppers:** Selfish pride keeps people from seeing what they can do to solve a problem. Equip people to pop pride with such pins as, "When I'm aggravated with someone else, I will deliberately look for what I can do to help."

•**Show the good in service:** Violence comes when we expect people to serve us and refuse to take responsibility for our actions. Encourage a positive view toward service by publicly praising behind the scenes service like keeping the nursery and serving in the kitchen (the original role of deacons according to Acts 6:1–3).

•**Highlight every member:** Conceit comes from having to prove oneself. If the church already recognizes each member, he or she will find it easier to be humble. Ways to recognize include: "Thank ____ for serving our church by ____" or by having a "member of the week." Include a line or two of appreciation with each.

•**Brainstorm ways to reduce anger:** Repaying evil for evil keeps the cycle of evil growing (Rom. 12:17–21). Together with your church list ways to stop the evil rather than keep it going. Let teams of four name one strategy for each letter of the alphabet. Then combine lists. For example: *A*nger means pain, so I talk about my pain rather than lash out; *B*asketball by myself to get out the angry feelings, so I'm calm enough to talk; *C*alm down by counting to 10, or 20, or 30; *D*irect my anger toward something I can't hurt, like writing in a journal.

•**Role-play two ways:** Invite church members to write circumstances that make them furious. Explain that you will shuffle these; then the group will act out a solution. Guide volunteers to role-play each circumstance in two ways: (1) the way people usually play it; and (2) the way God wants us to play it, with direct and problem-solving reactions.

•**Private testimonies:** Invite church members to write testimonies of ways God has helped them express violence-dissolving actions. Remove any identifying details before printing or reading them.

•**Practical preaching:** Ask your pastor to teach practical ways of growing family peace and preventing violence, woven around choosing to do the right thing for the people we love.

•**Peace pros:** In addition to your pastor and other teachers in your church, invite outside speakers who specialize in preventing violence and producing peace. Those outside our community can frequently say things in ways we receive more willingly.

•**Notice and highlight:** Quietly but deliberately notice when church members treat one another peacefully. "You talk to your friends so nicely—way to go!" or "I like the caring way you talk to your children in worship."

•**Communicate choice:** Assure church members that they can choose to create peace and defuse violence. It's not something that just happens or doesn't happen. Because God will help us, we can choose the caring action, the loving word, the loving attitude (Phil. 4:13,19). Patterns of peace grow as you choose to establish them. With God's help, choose peace rather than pain, using each word, action, and attitude: "He must turn from evil and do good; he must seek peace and pursue it" (1 Peter 3:11).

By practicing peace in our families and churches, we create more peaceful communities. The power to change the world begins in the church and in the home. When we actively become peacemakers, we can target specific problems caused by violence. The following chapter will heighten your awareness of the impact of violence on communities; subsequent chapters heighten your awareness of the impact of violence in our world. Each chapter will provide you with ministry models that have been successful in their peacemaking efforts. The following chapters also provide ideas you can implement in your family and community to make a better world.

Chapter Two

PURSUE PEACE IN COMMUNITIES

By Alvin Brooks

Violence is a way of life for many Americans. We all see, hear, or experience some kind of violence every day. It has, for many people, become acceptable behavior. More than 20,000 Americans die annually from homicides. Another 1.8 million are victims of other violent crimes each year.[1]

No community is untouched by violence. The most helpless are at greatest risk. Consider the following incidents, representing both large cities and smaller towns, the affluent and the poor, the old and the young.

A 2-year-old boy from Tampa died from a beating inflicted by his mother's boyfriend. The beating fractured his skull and caused his brain to swell. A previous court order had instructed the child's mother to keep her boyfriend away from the toddler after he was charged with beating him three months earlier.[2] The sad and short story of this child's life is repeated in communities across our nation. In 1995 alone, state child protective service (CPS) agencies investigations determined that more than 1 million children were victims of abuse or neglect.[3]

Sometimes those who abuse children are still children themselves. A 17-year-old girl from Philadelphia was sentenced to prison after giving birth in the shower and tucking the baby inside a gym bag, which she hid in her parents' garage. She did not tell anyone of the child's existence for

11

three days.[4] Criminologists expect juvenile crime to rise by 114 percent over the next decade.[5]

Gang activities generate many of the incidents of juvenile crime. In New York City, 27 members of the street gang known as the Crips were indicted on charges of conspiracy, attempted murder, sex abuse, and narcotic sales. According to the indictment, gang members protected their turf and drug activities through violence and intimidation, including death threats toward anyone who cooperated with the police. Those arrested ranged in age from 16 to 44.[6] Gang activity extends well beyond large cities like New York and Los Angeles. In Omaha, Nebraska, gangs were responsible for 41 percent of homicides in 1995. In Phoenix, Arizona, gang-related homicides jumped 800 percent between 1990 and 1994.[7] A law enforcement survey estimated that in 1991 there were 4,881 gangs with 249,324 members in existence in the United States.[8]

Like children, women are particularly vulnerable to violent assaults. A San Francisco man was charged with kidnapping his wife and transporting her across state lines while repeatedly assaulting, sexually abusing, and threatening to kill her. The incident began when his wife told him she was frightened by his increasing violence and wanted him to move out of their home. He reacted by shoving her down, hitting her in the face and stomach, threatening her with a knife, and choking her. The couple finally went to his mother's home in Florida. When his mother tried to intervene in the attacks, the man hit her with a lamp.[9] According to the US Department of Justice, women are the victims of more than 4.5 million violent crimes each year. In more than 29 percent of the violent crimes against women by lone offenders, the perpetrators were intimates—husbands, ex-husbands, boyfriends, or ex-boyfriends. Women with family incomes lower than $10,000 per year are more likely than other women to be attacked by an intimate.[10]

Women are also vulnerable to violent crimes in the form of sexual assaults. For example, Matthew James Morris, a 20-year-old, was sentenced to 21 years in prison in late 1997 after giving the illegal drug Rohyphol (a sedative known as the "date-rape pill") to a 15-year-old at a party and then raping her.[11] In the United States, 1.3 women are raped every minute. Sixty-one percent of all rape victims are younger than 18 years old. The United States has the world's highest rape rate of countries that publish such statistics—4 times that of Germany, 13 times higher than England, and 20 times higher than Japan.[12]

Poverty may well be the greatest contributor to the acts of violence women experience. Women head the majority of homeless families. In New York City's domestic violence programs, 59 percent of the women and children seeking shelter are turned away. About 50 percent of homeless women and children are fleeing abuse.[13] In 1996, the number of impoverished Americans was 36.5 million, representing 13.7 percent of the population.[14]

Another group at special risk for crime and violence is senior adults. Between 1986 and 1988, elder abuse reports increased by almost 20 percent nationally. Research indicates that only one in four elder abuse incidents are reported.[15]

A particular scourge of violence in America is racially motivated. An East Palo Alto, California, high school, Carlmont High, suspended two students and disciplined dozens of others for acts of racially motivated violence. They scrawled racist graffiti on the building, harassed minority students, and hurled obscenities at African-American and Hispanic students who were bused in from other parts of the city.[16] Of 7,947 hate crime incidents involving 10,469 victims in 1995, 61 percent were motivated by racial bias. Intimidation was the single most frequently reported offense.[17]

No place is immune to violence. Each week, an average of 20 workers are murdered and 18,000 are assaulted while at work or on duty.[18] More than 60 percent of workplace violence is in the form of verbal abuse, according to a study by the American Management Association. The US Department of Justice has added verbal abuse to its annual National Crime Victimization Survey.[19]

Americans do not direct their violence only at others. More people die from suicide than from homicide in the United States.[20] An air force pilot flew his bomb-laden warplane into the Rocky Mountains in early 1997. The pilot and his A-10 aircraft disappeared from the rear of a three-plane formation over Arizona and flew into Colorado some 850 miles off course. For three hours prior to the suicide, Button flew an erratic course in silence, out of communication with anyone on the ground.[21] On an average day, 84 people die from suicide and an estimated 1,900 adults attempt suicide.[22]

Prominent organizations and individuals in the field of mental health caution against automatically associating violence with mental health disturbances.[23] However, insanity (which is a legal term, not a psychiatric diagnosis) has been used in a number of criminal trials, including a 1996 trial. In that case, 38-year-old Mark Bechard was found not criminally responsible for stabbing and beating four nuns, resulting in the deaths of two. Bechard was diagnosed with schizo-affective disorder, which is marked by mood swings and hallucinations.[24]

Although the United States seeks to address violent assaults within its criminal justice system, that system also has its tragedies. Children who are 15 and older in Pennsylvania are automatically prosecuted as adults for crimes such as rape, robbery, or aggravated assault if they use a weapon or have a prior conviction for such crimes. An average of three teenagers per week goes to adult prison.[25] Over 40 percent of the increase in the prison population since 1980 is due to an increase in the prisoners convicted of violent offenses. The number of prisoners on death row continues to increase.[26]

While it seems less detrimental than its real-life counterpart, media violence is arguably the most pervasive and insidious. An American Medical Association trustee related the story of a family friend who was horribly beaten, raped, forced to drink a cleaning fluid, and finally shot in the back of the head during a robbery attempt in 1974. Once arrested, the killers explained they were emulating crime scenes from the movie *Magnum Force*, which they had watched a total of 22 times.[27] Children spend more time learning about life through television than in any other manner. The average child spends approximately 28 hours a week watching television, twice the amount of time they spend in school.[28] The average child will witness over 200,000 acts of violence on television, including 16,000 murders, before age 18.[29]

In addition to making ourselves aware of the profusion of violence in our nation, we can become involved in existing efforts or launch new efforts to curb it. As the examples in this book reveal, seemingly small steps such as painting over graffiti or offering a listening ear make a large impact. Everyone can do something to make the world a better place. We can and should begin in our homes and with our families. But we must not stop there. Concerned families can join with other families to extend their efforts into their communities.

Violent behavior is learned behavior. And if violence can be learned, peace can be learned as well. Adults must teach children and youth that violence is not acceptable behavior and model for them realistic alternatives to violence. A multitude of factors lead to violent behavior: poverty, substance abuse, drug trafficking, prejudice, racism, low self-esteem, long-held rage and uncontrolled emotions, frustration, hopelessness. And violence is more than a moral matter. It is a spiritual matter. Living life as God intends eliminates violence. When we are rightly connected to God, we enter into a reciprocal relationship with Him. This relationship, properly nurtured and maintained, prohibits us from causing pain and suffering to any of God's children.

BIBLICAL FOUNDATIONS

The Bible is clear in its accounts of God's expectations: God abhors and condemns violence. He promises and provides peace. He expects His followers to be promoters of peace. Both Old and New Testaments attest to these truths. The verses are strong and need little interpretation. Consider these:

"I will grant peace in the land, and you will lie down and no one will make you afraid. I will remove savage beasts from the land, and the sword will not pass through your country" (Lev. 26:6).

"Turn from evil and do good; seek peace and pursue it" (Psalm 34:14).

"The Lord gives strength to his people; the Lord blesses his people with peace" (Psalm 29:11).

"There is deceit in the hearts of those who plot evil, but joy for those who promote peace" (Prov. 12:20).

"'Peace, peace, to those far and near,' says the Lord. 'And I will heal them'" (Isa. 57:19b).

"The way of peace they do not know, there is no justice in their paths. They have turned them into crooked roads; no one who walks in them will know peace" (Isa. 59:8).

"Their children will be as in days of old, and their community will be established before me; I will punish all who oppress them" (Jer. 30:20).

"I will make a covenant of peace with them; it will be an everlasting covenant" (Ezek. 37:26a).

"I will take away the chariots from Ephraim and the war-horses from Jerusalem, and the battle bow will be broken. He will proclaim peace to the nations. His rule will extend from sea to sea and from the River to the ends of the earth" (Zech. 9:10).

"Salt is good, but if it loses its saltiness, how can you make it salty again? Have salt in yourselves, and be at peace with each other" (Mark 9:50).

"Peace I leave with you; my peace I give you. I do not give to you as the world gives. Do not let your hearts be troubled and do not be afraid" (John 14:27).

"I have told you these things, so that in me you may have peace. In this world you will have trouble. But take heart! I have overcome the world" (John 16:33).

"If it is possible, as far as it depends on you, live at peace with everyone" (Rom. 12:18).

"Let the peace of Christ rule in your hearts, since as members of one body you were called to peace. And be thankful" (Col. 3:15).

"Now may the Lord of peace himself give you peace at all times and in every way. The Lord be with all of you" (2 Thess. 3:16).

The prevalence of violence in American culture in no way suggests that God has failed. It suggests that we, as did God's people in the "days of the old," have failed God and have failed to emulate and follow His Son. Peace will not come to our communities until we become people of peace, pursue peace, and replace acts of violence with acts of peace. The biblical mandate is strong. We need to heed it.

SEEKING SOLUTIONS

Some Underlying Principles

How should the Christians in a community begin to pursue peace and thereby curb the violence that plagues us? Consider these principles:

•Make prayer the beginning, middle, and end of every day. The road to peace in individual lives, families, and communities is paved with prayer. You as an individual can help begin a spiritual renaissance in your community by praying for it. You can teach your children to pray for your community as well. And you can be the voice in your church that calls the church family to prayer for your community. A likely result will be your desire to put feet to your prayers and join God as He is at work around your community. That is God's desire and plan. He chooses to work through individuals who become aware, concerned, and available. We can live in homes, neighborhoods, and cities without violence. But we can't without God's help. We must commit as individuals to becoming peacemakers. And we must teach peacemaking skills to our children and grandchildren. Our homes should be havens of peace. When they are, our neighborhoods will, in turn, be safer from the threat of violence.

•**Work for justice rather than just assuming it will be granted.** Without justice there can be no peace. Respect the law enforcement and judicial systems that are in place, and teach that respect to your children. If some things are wrong, work within the system to correct them. Model good citizenship. Become knowledgeable about issues that affect your community, and be aware of how government leaders feel and plan to act concerning these issues. Use your voice, and join it with the voices of others to hold accountable those who are in elected positions of leadership. We are citizens of the heavenly kingdom, but God has also placed us in communities to be like salt and light, making a difference in positive ways.

•**Confront head-on the racism, bigotry, and prejudice that seek to alienate, belittle, and dehumanize people.** Unless Christians work against such attitudes, in our silence we help perpetuate them. Unless we work to destroy these attitudes, we allow them to pass from generation to generation. Christ represents peace. To be a Christian means to be like Christ. One cannot be racist, bigoted, or prejudiced and be Christlike. Prejudice is an opinion or judgment, usually unfavorable, formed beforehand, with no basis except personal feelings. Individual racism involves prejudice as well as power. Institutional racism involves the power of a dominant racial or ethnic group, excercised through the policies or practices of institutions, including churches, schools, governments, and businesses, to treat people indifferently or hurt them because of their race, ethnicity, or religion. Begin as an individual by broadening your circle of friends to include people of other races, cultures, beliefs, and income levels. Learn to respect them and their differences. Affirm the good you see in them. Model for the children you influence what inclusion, rather than exclusion, means.

•**Accept personal responsibility for the whole world, beginning in your community.** As a part of God's plan, He has given us a beautiful world with beautiful people, all of them made in His image. Because we are all God's children, the violence that affects one person or one group affects us all. God has entrusted the care of the world's people to us. We can assume responsibility for the world by first assuming responsibility in our homes, neighborhoods, schools, and communities, pursuing peace and promoting acts of love and concern rather than violence. Become an agent of change. Learn to take the initiative. Hold yourself and others accountable for what you have, who you know, and what you know. Instead of trying to assign blame for the problems violence brings to your community, become one who encourages and works to generate change. If you must point out a problem, attach a possible solution to it. Expect the best from yourself, your children, your spouse, your church, your schools, your government. Complacency provides an opening for the decay of peace and the onslaught of violence.

•**Don't panic.** Avoid using your valuable energy worrying about violence. Invest it instead in the pursuit peace. The remaining chapters in this book detail what you can do. Start somewhere. Start anywhere. But start!

Some Places to Begin

•Involve others in what you do. Beyond your family and even your church, seek out people who are aware of the needs in your community and want to make a difference. Cross racial, cultural, and denominational lines in cooperative ministry efforts. Recruit actively. Help people see the needs and assure them that their time will be well invested.

•Once you have a core group, assess the skills of those in the group. Get organized! Capitalize on the assets and strengths of those in the group. Affirm the potential contributions of each person. The person who answers the phone, keeps the files, or sweeps the floor is just as valuable and necessary as the one who directs the program, regardless of what it is. Plan both formal and informal ways to thank and recognize those who work with you.

•In addition to the other ways this book addresses to promote peace and curb violence, discover what exists in your community to help:

People with addictions to drugs and/or alcohol. Involve your volunteer group in the work of existing halfway houses. Consider beginning support groups. Plan ministries that target family members. Coordinate a communitywide educational campaign aimed at children and youth. Form a neighborhood council to promote education and awareness.

People with AIDS and their families. Often the victims of prejudice, isolation, ostracism, and even violence, people with AIDS and their families suffer emotionally as well as physically. Help set up buddy systems and support groups for them. Coordinate community awareness and education programs that will eliminate ignorance and prejudice.

People in need of social ministries. Discover the availability of emergency food pantries and clothes closets in your community. If none exist or you see the need, start some. Acts of family violence often result when parents feel hopeless, unable to meet the physical needs of their children. Also find out what exists in your area in the way of senior adult meal programs, children's clubs, youth programs, aerobics/exercise classes, mother's clubs, child care, after-school programs, health clinics, tutoring, children's choirs and music programs, and latchkey ministries.

Families in crisis. Find out what your community has to offer in the way of parent aide volunteers, parent support groups, mother's day out programs, parenting education, foster grandparents programs, and foster parenting programs. Consider beginning a ministry in one of these areas as a way to prevent family violence.

People who are homeless. Often easy targets for violent acts, homeless people are among society's most forgotten. Cooperate with other individuals, church groups, and community organizations as you make the lives of homeless people safer and work to move them into more permanent housing.

People who cannot read and write. A lack of education presents a host of problems, among them hopelessness. And this feeling can result in acts of violence. Explore existing literacy efforts in your community including adult reading and writing programs, English-as-a-second-language classes, and book banks. Involve your volunteer group in one of these worthwhile programs, or begin one where you see a need.

Clearly, one individual cannot stop the violence in his or her community. But one individual can make a difference. And that individual, working hand in hand with others, can become a strong force for peace and help put a stop to violence.

EXTEND THE WALLS OF THE CHURCH

By Brian Bakke

Our church congregation in urban Chicago is not unique, nor are we doing everything to respond to violence in our neighborhood. But we are directly addressing violence and responding to its root causes using the gifts of our church members. We have seen the power of God miraculously end fights and protect members in potentially dangerous situations.

Our neighborhood of Uptown is a small, densely populated enclave on Chicago's north side. Thousands of people live within its borders in thousands of subsidized low-income apartments. We have street people, mentally ill individuals, institutionalized adults, and homeless people who live alongside street gangs. There are less than a dozen evangelical churches, and almost all of these are relatively young. This community has become a human dumping ground for people living in chaos and unmanageability. Uptown Baptist Church is in the middle of this community and its chaos.

BIBLICAL FOUNDATIONS

In the midst of the violence which affects the Church, we must remember that we have a great promise on which to rely: "And . . . on this rock I will build my church, and the gates of Hades will not overcome it" (Matt. 16:18). Jesus made this promise to Peter during His ministry here on earth. He went on to promise: "I will give you the keys of the kingdom of heaven; whatever you bind on earth will be bound in heaven; whatever you loose on earth will be loosed in heaven." No matter what occurs in the temporal realm, we know that God has promised the Church that what He has built, not with bricks and mortar, but with His gospel, will stand.

From God's Word, we also know that today's churches are not the only ones to experience hardship and violence. Early churches were subject to great persecution (Acts 8:1,3). Early Christians responded to persecutions and violence with God's love (Acts 7:59). The spiritual principle of turning the other cheek rather than responding in kind can neutralize the venom of violence (Luke 22:50–51; Prov. 15:1).

While God does not expect us to respond to violence with violence, He neither expects believers to remain complacent in its face. We see the peace that one believer (Acts 9:28–31) and the power of prayer (Acts 12:5–7) can bring. God abhors violence (Gen. 6:11). We can be peacemakers here on earth, doing His work, diminishing violence through prayer and acts of love. Following are some methods which have been effective in our church's ministry, and which are adaptable for other church communities.

SEEKING SOLUTIONS

• Change the External Church Environment.

As a church, we began reclaiming the neighborhood by taking back our own front steps. Nightly drinking parties, drug dealing, and prostitution created enough refuse to fill a city garbage can with used bottles, condoms, and human waste. First we tried sending teams of laypeople out on the steps as witness-intervention teams. This failed because the people on the steps didn't want to talk to us; they just wanted to drink and take drugs. They would leave when they saw us coming and return after we'd gone. After 3 years of debate, we decided to put a gate across our steps and across the yards. We also put in new landscaping and a garden. The effects were immediate. The parties moved elsewhere. Our corner became much more peaceful. Neighbors came to us and thanked us for making our corner safe, saying that they were afraid to walk past the church before.

• Change the Internal Church Environment.

We discourage inappropriate behavior inside our church by displaying signs that state expected behavior. Our ushers know to remove unruly attendees from services. At special events, we station people at the doors to prevent those who want to disrupt and destroy. Unfortunately, that is all some people are interested in doing, and there are some people we have actually had to bar from our building. We keep a list of such people on hand. We used to have a pay phone in our church, but we had it turned off because drug dealers were using it. They also regularly used the five pay phones at the intersection by our church. One of our elders met with our city council member and asked that she use her office to remove these phones. She didn't support this, so we called the national headquarters of the franchises that licensed the phones and told them that their businesses in Uptown had a reputation for harboring crime. The phones eventually left our corner. At the same time, we invited the police to come into our building and use our church's tower for surveillance on drug dealing and street violence.

• Form Community Organizations.

The parking lot of the fast-food restaurant across the street from our church hosted a large number of drug arrests, and our community rated high for prostitution arrests. After studying this problem, we attacked on several fronts. First, we sponsored large public meetings where residents voiced their concerns about safety and increasing violence. Then we got active in starting block clubs. These are organized groups of neighbors who meet for the express purpose of taking back their streets. Several lay members immediately rose into key leadership positions in these groups, which have networked sections of the community. They meet regularly with police captains and officers who patrol the beats.

The club members have started phone chains, where not one call, but dozens of calls to 911 hit the police at the same time. This has dramatically improved police response time and has created a network around the entire community. One of our members who was the leader of one of these block clubs is now an elected public official. She is using her office to attack crime and remove criminals from the streets.

• Work Through Legal Venues.

Our church has been the leader in a grassroots effort to address public drinking. Our neighborhood has been making effective use of a little-known Chicago law that allows election precincts to vote themselves "dry," or alcohol-free. It takes a lot of organization and encouragement because the alcohol industry doesn't appreciate our attention. They spend a great deal of time and money to frustrate, confuse, and intimidate people from following through with their actions. We went to court to fight for the right to put the question before voters and hold an election. Then we went to court to fight to uphold the election results. In our first case, the court battles took almost 3 years as the issue went all the way to the state court of appeals. Our goal for an alcohol-free community will take years to become a reality due to the proliferation of liquor stores and bars in the immediate neighborhood. But we have seen several liquor stores close already. Peace and quiet now reign where drinking orgies and continuous fighting used to be commonplace.

• Minister to Community Needs.

Our church has opened our building to at-risk youth and gang members so that they can hear the gospel message and have opportunities for Christian discipleship. Our basement has a small weight room with dumbbells and barbells. Several men and youth leaders invite youth into the gym to lift weights together. One of our next steps is to open a full-scale "God's Gym" in the basement that will target local youth and gang members. While in the gym they can listen to Christian music and work out with older brothers in Christ who are experienced in both physical and spiritual body building. Our focus is evangelism, and one of the positive outcomes is that problematic individuals get off the street and come into the church.

For the first 15 years of our church's history we had no men's ministry. Fathers have a God-given responsibility to teach their children about godly living, but for the most part the men of our community were teaching their children that to be a man was to avoid responsibility. This may be the single greatest reason for violence in the city today—youth grow up without learning how to be godly men and women. Since many fathers abdicate this responsibility, children and youth make up their own rules as they go along. Life becomes cheap as they learn to love things and use people. This trend became a burden on some of our church's elders and pastors.

Sensing God's timing, the pastor made a leap of faith and purchased tickets to a Promise Keepers rally on his credit card. Almost 30 men piled into cars and vans and took a road trip to Detroit. Upon the group's return, the pastor asked 2 of the men to start a discipleship ministry targeting men. A group of 4 men began meeting in a glorified closet in our church's basement, studying one or two verses at a time from the Book of James. Nine months later the group numbered over 20 active men. The following year 65 men went to a Promise Keepers rally in Chicago.

Today our ministry to men challenges them to live biblical lives marked by the fruits of the Spirit. We train them to be Sunday School teachers and small-group leaders, ushers, future deacons, and elders. This men's group includes African-American, Asian, Hispanic, and Anglo men of all ages, some of whom have seminary degrees and some of whom live in shelters. Our vision is to seed our neighborhood with men who have been redeemed from lives of chaos and violence and send them into the community.

Our church is a cofounder and active leader in an ecumenical evangelical ministry called the Miracle League. It began in 1991 when several gang members approached a church staff member outside his home and said, in effect, "If you give us a place to go, we'll get off your corner. There is a church gym down the street, and you're a church man, so maybe you can work something out. We love basketball." Three people from 2 churches got together and started praying and dreaming. They set out to invite every church in their part of the city to join together in cooperative ministry. They invited 60 churches, and 3 responded. While they prayed for an army of volunteers, only a few got involved.

Since then, the Miracle League has grown to involve over a dozen churches in traditions ranging from Mennonite to charismatic, and has seen rival street gangs come together across turf lines for Bible study, prayer, and basketball. We have seen God work in powerful ways through this ministry, with almost half the teams being coached by young men who have been mentored and discipled by their coaches. It has clearly earned its name, the Miracle League.

The gangs in our neighborhood have, in a way, been instrumental in a rather unique opportunity to get in the way of Satan's desires. A couple of church members were involved in a private war against gang graffiti. They began getting up early in the mornings to paint over the gang slogans with white paint. The walls they whitewashed lasted for a week or so. But before long, gang members would again tag them, claiming segments of the community as their turf. One of the whitewash painters was an artist, and he asked some of the gang members if they would like to do a mural on a specific wall.

"Would it be real religious, like 'Believe in Jesus,' or 'Trust in Jesus,' something like that?" the gang members wanted to know.

"Sure, I guess so," the artist responded.

After a pause a gang member said, "Well, that sounds OK, but I'll bring it up at the meeting next week."

The painter was surprised but hopeful and began praying about this new idea.

The gang not only gave permission for their own graffiti to be covered, but stated they would protect the wall from anyone else who might deface the image. The church now has an active mural ministry averaging eight murals a year in and around the neighborhood. In every case where a large outdoor wall covered with gang graffiti has been repainted—usually with the enthusiastic help of youth and children from the community—the response has been overwhelmingly positive. Most people have really enjoyed the murals' beauty and message. We have seen a marked reduction in drug trafficking and violence. One street, which had seven shootings in the spring prior to the mural, now has peace. No longer do rival gangs or gang members and police engage in shoot-outs there.

Another very simple but effective antiviolence measure our church members have taken involves active removal of litter on their street. Gangs and drug dealers were known to hide drugs and weapons in the street litter. Our members sweep the streets and pick up knives, pipes, bricks, boards, and bottles that might otherwise be used as weapons. Since the main drug-hiding spots are kept clean, some of the drug dealers have moved to other places. We have actually seen gangs leave when a mature Christian comes out on the street armed with prayer and a broom!

Your community may be very different from ours, but the chances are great that it is marked by violence. Whether random or frequent, in small communities or inner cities, violence breaks God's heart. Where is your church when violence rears its ugly head? What is your church's response? What should be your church's response? While you cannot do everything, you can do something. Help your church become a beacon of hope and light that diminishes the violence around it.

Chapter Four

CARE FOR, LOVE, AND PROTECT CHILDREN

By Erlene Grise-Owens

Violence affects children more than any other population group, because they inherit the legacy of all the violence this book addresses. Some children do not remember a time when violence seemed unusual.

By the time the typical child begins middle school, he or she has witnessed more than 8,000 murders and 100,000 acts of violence on television.[1] The effects of violent television are myriad, causing children to expect, accept, and enact violence. The more children view television violence, the more they see the world as scary and hostile, see violence as acceptable behavior, and imitate violent behavior.[2] Most children have diminishing beliefs that the world is safe, developing what Mary Pipher calls the "mean world syndrome."[3]

Today, children are bombarded with violent toys, games, and media. Instead of an occasional taste of violence, children consume a constant diet of violent fare. Popular video games like Mortal Kombat are regular courses. In this game, the player rips out the heart and cuts off the head of his opponent, all of which is depicted in vivid imagery.[4] Although the effects of video games have not been fully studied, many experts believe they are even more harmful than passively watching television violence. With video games, children actively participate by pushing buttons; they win and are rewarded by destroying people.[5]

Along with the excessive entertainment violence children experience, astonishing numbers of children experience personal violence on a daily basis. The US Department of Health and Human Services reports that the abuse and neglect of children nearly doubled between 1986 and 1993.[6] Generally, abuse is defined as a nonaccidental act resulting in injury or harm; neglect is defined as failure to provide for a child's needs resulting in harm. In 1993, the estimated number of abused and neglected children rose to 2.81 million. These figures represent a rise in the problem's severity, rather than simply a heightened awareness and increased reporting of abuse and neglect.[7]

While the number of severely abused and neglected children continues to rise, most public agencies are understaffed and under-resourced. Likewise, most private agencies, such as children's homes and family services agencies, are under-resourced and unable to respond adequately to the needs.

A number of factors contribute to child abuse and neglect, including family isolation, a history of family violence, poverty, substance abuse, and a lack of healthy parenting skills. Although the rates tend to be higher for low-income and single-parent families, children in all types of families experience abuse and neglect. Child abuse most often occurs from people the child knows—particularly parents and primary caregivers. Of children who are killed, 54 percent die at the hands of family members; only 6 percent die at the hands of strangers.[8]

A significant contributor to violence against children in the US is the proliferation of handguns. In 1993, 116 preschoolers died by gunfire—more than the number of police officers or American soldiers killed in the line of duty that same year.[9] While the home should be a safe place, a gun in the home is 43 times more likely to be used to kill a family member than a stranger.[10]

BIBLICAL FOUNDATIONS

Even the most cursory Bible study reveals the importance God gives to children! Some of the most tender and powerful metaphors describing God's relationship with us compare the relationship to that of parent and child (Psalm 103:13; Isa. 66:13). Underlying these metaphors is the assumption that we are to care for, love, and protect children.

The Bible teaches us to relate to God in the manner of a child; furthermore, our response to children demonstrates our commitment as Christians. Using the image of a child to illustrate God's desired relationship with people is a prime example of the value God places on children (Matt. 18:1–5).

The familiar biblical passage, "Jesus said, 'Let the little children come to me, and do not hinder them, for the kingdom of heaven belongs to such as these'" (Matt. 19:13–14), reminds us that Jesus specifically took time for children. He did this in spite of a culture in which a busy schedule and adult demands were held with more importance.

Certainly Jesus knew of the abuse, neglect, and violence suffered by children, and He registered grave warnings against anyone who caused harm to children (Luke 17:2). In this warning, Jesus tacitly admonishes Christians to correct situations that harm children. Essentially, if we abdicate our responsibility to children, we abdicate our relationship to God. Zechariah 8:5 envisions a community living the will of God in which all—but perhaps particularly the children—are safe. This vision is not some distant and unreachable goal, but rather God's call to us to fulfill this vision and create a world where "children can play in the streets."

These passages direct us to value and care for children. Looking at these passages and the world in which children live leads us to consider a response as individuals, families, churches, communities, and a nation.

SEEKING SOLUTIONS

Ministry Models

Concerned Christians are involved in a variety of programs and ministries to address the violence that affects today's children. This section briefly highlights a sampling of the numerous programs that are making a difference. These programs support the idea that every individual, every family, every church, and every community can address the problem of children and violence. One of the most effective ways to promote nonviolence is to offer safe and positive alternatives.

The Preschool Partners program is a partnership between St. Luke's Episcopal Church and the Birmingham Baptist Association in Birmingham, Alabama. Preschool Partners offers a five-day-a-week program of preschool education for children in low-income areas for families with limited options. The program requires that one of the child's parents attend weekly half-day sessions. These sessions concentrate on helping parents improve their own reading skills and learn positive discipline and other parenting skills. While the program's primary focus is preschool education, a positive by-product is the parents' support network. Parents often develop friendships and share child care, thus reducing the isolation they may feel. While not an explicitly identified goal of the program, Preschool Partners reduces child abuse and neglect in the community by reducing some of the factors that lead to abuse.[11]

Mt. Pleasant Baptist Church in Kansas City, Missouri, operates a summer Freedom School for children, using college students as mentor-teachers. It, too, has significant parent involvement. Twenty-eight similar schools last year kept over 2,000 children involved in positive, nonviolent activities.[12]

A partnership between parents, churches, businesses, and law enforcement in Akron, Ohio, succeeded in getting 1,500 guns off the streets through a coordinated "gun buy-back." Businesses offered coupons for free merchandise in exchange for turning in a gun. Foundations gave grants for cash to buy back guns. Churches held special worship services, posted banners listing names of children lost to gunfire, and offered speech contests with monetary rewards on the subject "Kids and Guns Don't Mix." This effort raised the community's awareness of the dangers of handguns, made the city safer for children, and provided opportunities for churches to give witness to their commitment to children.[13]

St. Agatha Family Empowerment (SAFE) is a multi-faceted program of the St. Agatha parish, a Chicago neighborhood with high levels of violence. SAFE offers a "litany of activities" for children, including sports, choir, theater, and tutoring. One measure of SAFE's success is that 100 percent of its participants graduate from high school in a neighborhood where 55 percent of the teenagers are high school dropouts. SAFE also involves teenagers in planning and running children's activities and teaching them leadership and responsibility.[14]

Plan A

The magnitude and urgency of the problem of children and violence calls for immediate response—it calls for Plan A! Plan A involves attitude, awareness, advocacy, and action.

Undergirding and infusing all the steps in Plan A is *attitude*. Our attitudes must remain prayerful. And this requires that we remain open to the revelation of God for responding creatively to this issue; that we rely on faith to address an overwhelming situation; and that we acknowledge that we need the unfailing help of God and the help of our sisters and brothers in Christ. It also requires personal prayer: making prayer for children an integral part of our community ministry and beginning prayer groups around children's concerns with other church members and other faith communities.

You are already on the road to *awareness* because you are reading this book! But we must also become familiar with the issues of children and violence in the local community. Learn about the child abuse reporting policies in your community by contacting local child welfare agencies (e.g., children's homes), child-care agencies, other social service agencies, or the local police department. Ask someone to speak about needs, current interventions, and ways the church can become involved in promoting nonviolence and protecting children.

Children affected by violence cannot speak for themselves. Therefore, we are called to *advocacy* for them—being the voice of the silent victims of violence. The Bible instructs us to "speak out for those who cannot speak, for the rights of all the destitute. Speak out, judge righteously, defend the rights of the needy" (Prov. 31:8). You can become an advocate by:

- calling for legislative policies which prioritize and protect children, as well as policies providing persons who work with children with livable wages and adequate resources;
- encouraging churches and other community entities caring for children to have policies protecting children and to have training on recognizing child abuse;
- encouraging churches to prioritize children's needs in programming and finances;
- voicing displeasure through letters and telephone calls to businesses that promote violent media, video games, and toys and entertainment industries, such as television networks, that promote violence;
- showing support of positive products and programming;
- joining or beginning a child advocacy group at the local, state, or national level;
- voting with priority on children's concerns;
- sponsoring a children's issues forum with political candidates;
- participating in the Children's National Sabbath, the Stand for Children March, or other activities which call attention to and raise commitment for children.

To be most effective, Plan A calls for *action*—involving ourselves in activities that make the world safer for children, such as:

- offering tutoring, recreation, mentoring, Bible clubs, and other similar opportunities;
- becoming a Big Brother/Big Sister;

•becoming a foster family or a respite foster family;

•adopting a special-needs child who has suffered neglect and abuse, or supporting a family to do so;

•turning off the television and turning children on to reading;

•providing a workshop or distributing information about gun violence and children;

•sponsoring an essay, speech, and/or art contest on peace-making for children;

•beginning a parent support group in your community;

•starting a latchkey program in your community, such as a "warm line" for children to call for a caring adult's support after school;

•cleaning up and patrolling a local park that is unsafe for children;

•adopting a local school, homeless shelter, social service agency, or an employee in one of these agencies;

•providing scholarships for children to go to camp;

•serving on or beginning an antiviolence/safety committee in your community to speak for children in particular;

•creating a newsletter dedicated to raising awareness about children's needs and/or using other church mediums to communicate about children's issues;

•beginning a Peace and Justice Committee with particular attention to children's issues, and including children on this committee;

•providing affordable, quality day care in your community and/or supporting day cares already in operation.

Sadly, the violence in our communities, nation, and world touches every child. The good news is that we can make a difference by intervening with any and all children.

The ideas suggested above are examples of the myriad of ways to be involved. Most experts agree that one of the keys to success in promoting nonviolence is collaboration. Find out what is already being done in your community to combat the violence that touches children. Then join with that, contributing your unique part in creating a nonviolent community for children.

Chapter Five

NURTURE AND EQUIP YOUTH

By Ken Goode

Two mothers wept and a community grieved—again. One mother wept because her beautiful teenaged daughter, the victim of a gunshot wound, would never again come home. The other mother grieved because her son would not be coming home for a long time. He sat instead in a concrete box of a cell in the county jail. His were the actions that were responsible for the girl's death.

American youth both live in and help to create a violent world. Though the violence may not always be as extreme as the incident that opens this chapter, youth experience violence both as victims and as perpetrators. Theirs is a world enveloped by what William DeJong calls, "a culture of violence."[1] Statistics paint a troubling picture. Since 1979, more than 50,000 people younger than 20 have been killed violently in the United States. This figure far exceeds the battle casualties of the Vietnam War.[2] Youth younger than 18 are responsible for 20 percent of our nation's violent crime.[3] Juvenile killings with firearms increased fourfold from 1984 to 1994.[4] Homicide is the leading cause of death for African-American males.[5] The Children's National Medical Center in Washington, DC, experienced a 1,740 percent increase in penetrating trauma caused by violence between 1986 and 1989.[6]

Because homicide statistics are the most readily available, they are most often used to paint the canvas of teenage violence. The bulk of the canvas, however, is painted with the untold incidents of nonfatal fights, assaults, and other acts of aggression. One study suggests that the number of assaults is 100 times higher than the number of homicides.[7]

Violence occurs in every domain of youth's existence, including the place they are most concentrated—our schools. A 700-city survey by the National League of Cities found that school violence had increased significantly in 40 percent of the surveyed cities, two-thirds of which were cities with a population of less than 50,000.[8] Mark Sanders reported the results of a survey of 65,000 6th to 12th grade students that revealed these statistics: every school day 160,000 students avoid a class because of fear of harm; 20,000 students are physically attacked at school on a regular basis; and 81 percent of students surveyed said they would be happier if they felt safe at school.[9]

This culture of violence results in devastating consequences for our youth, their families, their communities, and society at large. Its economic, emotional, and human toll is high. One of its consequences is the erosion "of the soil that children need to grow," and the threat to "every aspect of their development."[10]

BIBLICAL FOUNDATIONS

Abandonment, isolation, unpredictability, insecurity, and hopelessness color the turbulent, violent world of America's youth. Theirs is a world often removed from the world of the church. Unquestionably, youth violence can thrust itself into the life of the church, but the church is not its domain. Its domain is in other places where the church is reluctant to go. Consequently, if the church is going to make an impact on our society's experience of youth violence, it must thrust itself into these other domains.

An incident in the history of the Israelite exodus, recorded in Numbers 16, gives the contemporary church direction in penetrating these other domains. The story opens with the account of Korah, son of Levi, leading 250 Israelite leaders in rebellion against Moses and Aaron. This mob of leaders confronted Moses and Aaron and, in essence, said, "Moses and

Aaron, who died and made you the boss?" Quickly they found that it was God Who had called Moses and Aaron to their positions. God opened the earth for judgment and it swallowed the rebellious group.

This act of judgment riled the rest of the nation of Israel so that they too rebelled against Moses and Aaron. Instead of resting in the satisfaction of God's threat of judgment on the people, Moses and Aaron fell on their faces before God and begged for mercy for the people (v. 45). Moses commanded Aaron to run to the altar and make a sacrifice of atonement for the people. Aaron took the sacrifice and made his stand "between the living and the dead" (v. 48).

Notice the critical place he took his stand. He did not take his stand in the tabernacle, nor did he retreat to his prayer closet. He took his stand in the assembly (v. 46). He did not go *to* but *into* the congregation; he penetrated their presence. This principle is an important one for the Christian church. We must penetrate the lives of violence-affected youth. That cannot happen most effectively strictly within the walls of the church. The streets, the schools, the families of youth, treatment and correctional institutions, and gathering places of youth must see and feel the presence of the church.

To take a stand between the dead and the living, the church must meet the youth in their territory. This is not a comfortable place to go. It is a place where the church can see the beauty of life and the ugliness of death; feel the hope of life and the pain of death; hear the anthem of life and the dirge of death; and smell the incense of life and the stench of death. It is the place where hope stares hopelessness in the face and claims life over death.

SEEKING SOLUTIONS

Ministry Models

Repainting the canvas of youth violence requires an understanding of the factors that create the picture. The factors are numerous and interrelated, but they can be grouped into two categories: individual and environmental. The individual category includes factors rooted in the youth and the youth's family. Consider that:

•Substance abuse in the home and the resultant substance abuse by youth play a major role in violent behavior. Alcohol is a factor in 65 percent of homicides and a factor in 55 percent of assaults in the home.[11]
•Lack of parental supervision is a strong contributor to violent behavior.[12]
•Violence in the home creates the perception that violence is a normal behavior.[13]
•Child abuse in the home (including sexual, physical, and emotional abuse, and neglect) increases the likelihood of violent behavior in youth.[14]
•School failure is a strong predictor of violent behavior.

The environmental category includes factors rooted in community and society:

•The easy availability of firearms creates injuries and fatalities in otherwise nonlethal situations.
•Chronic violence in the community conditions youth to violent behavior.
•Media violence through television and video games is a "significant factor" in violent behavior.[15]
•The presence of gangs in a community increases violence.
•Poverty creates social stresses that contribute to violence.

When a ministry or program positively impacts any of these factors, violence is reduced. Consider these ministry models, and notice how each addresses factors that contribute to violence.

•College Park Baptist Church is located in the economically deprived, ethnically mixed old part of Las Vegas. The church addressed the need for a safe place for youth by opening its doors to the students from the high school across the street. The church served a low-cost lunch and showed Christian videos during the students' lunch period. As many as 300 students came for lunch. On Friday nights from 7:00 P.M. to 12:00 midnight, the church opens its recreation area for Bible study, recreational activities, and special events. According to the former director of these programs, Linda King, they help youth at risk for violence "get past the idea that church is a bad place to be." They teach youth from a variety of backgrounds and gang affiliations that they can get along.

• The Wise Men and Women program is a multicultural mentorship program sponsored by Youth Development Incorporated in Albuquerque, New Mexico. This program seeks to decrease the potential of violence in the school and community by increasing the academic and social success of students. Adult mentors are placed in the school to work with two to four children on a weekly basis, spending 30 minutes a week with each child. In that time, the mentor is able to teach social, academic, and life skills and provide encouragement to the child. Teachers have observed an increase in self-esteem and academic performance in the students involved with the program. (For more information contact Kenneth J. Carson, Sr., Wise Men and Women, 1016 Juan Tabo NE, Albuquerque, NM 87112-5800; [505] 271-2066.)

• The South Broadway community of Albuquerque allied itself with some of the churches in the community to launch an effort against the drug dealing and youth violence that was destroying the neighborhood. The movement, known as Peace in the Streets, was a grassroots effort to mobilize neighbors to take a stand against destructive forces in the community. The churches became the rallying points for neighbors as they organized marches to put drug dealers and violent youth on notice that their illegal activity would no longer be tolerated. Out of the marches grew working relationships with law enforcement, city officials, city departments, and politicians. These relationships produced an organized process to empower the community and to decrease the incidents of youth violence in the community.

Some Places to Begin

Approaches that will repaint the canvas of youth violence range from complex to simple. One group of approaches involves *creating awareness* of the problem. Individuals and churches can:

•Teach a biblical model of conflict resolution to youth and parents.
•Educate parents and youth about the role substance abuse and firearms play in youth violence.
•Promote activities and events in the church and community that will decrease opportunities for violence.

Individuals and churches can also advocate *policy and system changes*. They can:

•Use the political process to advocate controls on the sales of alcohol.
•Use the political system to advocate gun safety and/or gun control.
•Advocate needed policy changes in areas like housing, businesses, and schools.

Approaches that bring *change to the physical and social environment* form another group of responses. Individuals and churches can:

•Organize the community to speak out against violence and the factors that cause violence.
•Create safe, affordable housing.
•Provide a job bank for unemployed youth and adults.
•Create small businesses and other jobs.
•Make health care accessible to youth and their families.
•Clean up schools, empty lots, streets, parks, and other areas.
•Keep the church facility in good repair and keep parking and pedestrian areas well lit.
•Lead youth to clean, paint, and repair community residences.

•Encourage landscaping that decreases dangerous blind spots and promotes an atmosphere of peace and harmony.

•Encourage church members to become community volunteers in schools, medical facilities, correctional facilities, civic organizations, and community organizations.

A final group of approaches can equip youth and their families to live with fewer risk factors for violence. Individuals and churches can:

•Host sports programs that provide controlled activities.
•Offer recreational activities, especially during times when violence is likely to occur (for example, midnight basketball).
•Learn the name of an ignored or isolated youth and speak to him or her.
•Develop a tutoring program.
•Teach self-defense classes.
•Teach hobby classes such as model building, cooking, leather crafting, sewing, car repair, bicycling, or fishing.
•Teach art and music classes.
•Teach job hunting skills to parents and youth.
•Teach anger management.
•Play basketball with the youth down the street or in the park.
•Sponsor career fairs.
•Create safe havens in the church and homes where youth can flee from trouble.
•Write letters to youth in correctional facilities and mental health facilities.
•Offer parenting classes.
•Offer camping experiences for troubled youth.
•Love your children.

Everybody can do something to brush a stroke in repainting the canvas of youth violence.

Guidelines for Building Relationships

A relationship is the most effective tool for working with and witnessing to youth involved in or affected by violence. It is the tool God used to reach humanity. He became flesh and dwelt among us. Building a productive relationship requires love, patience, and determination. These guidelines will be helpful in developing a relationship:

Do not probe for information. A characteristic of many of these youth is a deep lack of trust in anybody outside their circle of relationships. Asking a lot of questions may raise suspicion that you are more interested in what they know than who they are. Let the information flow as the relationship grows.

Do not make promises you cannot keep. You will hear stories of incredibly needy and broken lives. The instinctive reaction is to try to fix the problems, but the problems are complex and difficult to solve. Do not get involved in the problems to the extent that you make commitments you cannot keep. Broken commitments erode trust.

Do not try to talk and act like the youth unless it is natural to you. Be yourself.

Decide ahead of time what information you will keep confidential. As the relationship grows, you will see and hear things you should report to authorities. Decide beforehand what you will do with information concerning criminal behavior, child abuse, and potential harm to self or others. As early as possible in the relationship, make very clear to the youth what types of information you need to report.

If you make a mistake, apologize. Mistakes and bad judgments occur in every relationship. When it happens, apologize. This will rebuild trust. Simply apologize; do not grovel.

Be patient about relationships. Let trust grow naturally. Remember that trusting relationships allow opportunities to minister.

Respect the youth. Look for their strengths, not their weaknesses. Build on their strengths.

Work through the relapses. Just when you think you are making progress, there may be regression. Do not excuse it, but let the youth know you are there to help them get back up.

Accept people where they are. Profanity and other behavior may make you uncomfortable. Do not become so focused on these that you find yourself constantly preaching. Through your constant example, nurture youth toward more acceptable behavior.

Chapter Six

DIMINISH THE LURE OF GANGS

By Ann Putnam Grelling

Many people immediately associate the concept of violence with the image of gangs—young men roaming the streets of inner-city neighborhoods in metropolitan areas, terrorizing everyone in their path. But this is only a partial view both of violence and of gangs, and such an incomplete concept allows many to believe that gangs are someone else's problem.

Gangs infest large cities, but they also find homes in smaller towns and suburbs across our country. "Gangs can be found in suburban cities with populations as small as 5,000."[1] "In 1991, more than 700 cities reported gang activity; that's up from 54 cities in 1960."[2] Cities like Charlottesville, Virginia; Beaumont, Texas; Little Rock, Arkansas; Birmingham, Alabama; and Nashville, Tennessee, display the graffiti and experience the violence associated with gangs. Even rural communities attach drugs and crime to gang connections.

Whether in the inner-city or the suburbs, what defines a group of people as a gang? A generally accepted definition is a group of individuals with an identifiable membership who engage in illegal and antisocial behavior. Gangs generally have a geographical territory or turf that they control and defend. Often they form along ethnic lines. But for some, profits from drug sales outweigh other loyalties, causing membership to cross ethnic lines. Females have always been related to gangs, but exclusively female gangs are not uncommon and represent a growing trend. Crime and antisocial behavior constitute the common bond for all gangs. Gang members consider themselves outlaws.

45

Initiation into gangs frequently involves crime. Potential gang members generally must commit a specific crime such as robbery, drive-by shooting, rape, or assault to prove their worth and loyalty to the gang. Once youth are entrenched in gangs, they engage in violence and crime as a way of life, with little thought of their consequences. Many gang members do not expect to live long, so the possibility of death is not a great deterrent for their criminal behaviors.

With the problem so ugly and foreign to most people, why should Christians become involved? Consider the innocent victims of gang-related crimes, the loss of potential of young people who are drawn into gangs, and the fact that few communities are immune from gangs. And here's a compelling fact: we *can* make a difference.

The Christian community can make a difference because we can address many of the reasons children and youth are vulnerable to gangs. Many are lonely, have little sense of belonging, and view themselves and their futures with hopelessness. Gangs become family for them and provide a sense of belonging, safety, identity, and status. The needs that these represent are not wrong or unhealthy. But the family, church, and community in which many young people live do not meet these needs in a healthy way. Christians can provide healthy, appropriate solutions to these needs. Many young people related to gangs want a way out. Many will respond to offers of hope, direction, leadership, structure, and love. And for everyone we reach, there is one less gang recruiter to entice young children into the gang lifestyle.

Many communities are only now beginning to recognize some of the warning signs of possible gang activity, such as graffiti, drugs, and weapons. If concerned Christians work together to deal with initial manifestations of these problems, gangs will find it difficult to maintain a stronghold in communities and schools.

Perhaps the most important reason Christians can and should make an effort to diminish the lure of gangs is because the good news we have to offer is better than what gangs have to offer. Our God is stronger than any evil.

BIBLICAL FOUNDATIONS

God must view gang activity with a broken heart. Habakkuk 2:8 records God's word of judgment to His people who "have shed man's blood; you have destroyed lands and cities and everyone in them." This description could just as easily paint a picture of today's communities in which the evil of gangs grows unchecked. God's intent for His people is that they be a blessing to others and that they "seek the peace and prosperity of the city to which I have carried you into exile" (Jer. 29:7a). God places us in communities not to live in isolation, but to live as part of the communities. Within a community, God calls us to be salt and light, to be His presence, and to bring His kingdom's influence to bear on that environment. While gangs affect entire communities, individuals most directly feel the hurt. Jesus, by His example and His words, taught us to love all people and minister to their needs. Evidences of our own salvation, according to Matthew 25, are our acts of compassion toward people in prison, in need of basic physical resources, and in need of friendship. Through Jesus' own declaration of His ministry, He defined His calling: "Preach good news to the poor . . . proclaim freedom for the prisoners . . . recovery of sight for the blind, to release the oppressed" (Luke 4:18).

As Christ's followers and representatives, these are our ministries, too. God calls us in Christ to reach out to people who are oppressed or held captive by their circumstances. Few words better describe the young people, families, and communities affected by gang activities than *oppressed* and *captive*. Individuals are captives in their homes, fearful of gang violence. Helplessness and hopelessness heavily oppress families whose children are drawn into gangs and their futures. Their lives are placed in jeopardy.

Young people in communities where gangs have a stronghold often join gangs for their own survival, seeking to avoid intimidation tactics. Once involved, they become captives to a lifestyle that culminates in the loss of potential for a productive life, conflict with law enforcement agencies, even death. Each of these young people is someone for whom

Christ died. Each is someone to whom Christ sends us to share the love and redemption that can loosen their bonds (Matt. 28:19–20).

Our mandate involves showing Christ's love not just in words, but "with actions and in truth" (1 John 3:18). That means developing ministries and approaches that allow us to build relationships through which we can communicate love. Relationships are necessary and important to God, Who ultimately chose relationships as the way to reveal Himself. Fundamental to our knowledge of Christ is our understanding of His incarnation. God in Christ chose to come, dwell among us, and relate to us (John 1:14). God in Christ was willing to know us and show His love to us in a direct and personal relationship. He calls us as Christians to relate to others in the same way and share with them His good news of life and redemption. The Bible also teaches that every person is created in the image of God and has worth in His sight. This not only dictates that we do ministries but also affects what ministries we do and how we do them. Our ministries should empower people to reach their full potential and become all that God envisioned when He created them. We should respect the people with whom we minister, involve them in planning the ministry, and learn from them. Our focus should be on ministry *with* others rather than ministry *to* others. By joining with our neighbors and working with them, we can reclaim our communities from gangs and the violence they encourage. By showing others, particularly children and youth, the value each person has in God's eyes and therefore in ours, we can help instill in them self-worth. Armed with the assurance of their value to God and the potential they have, they can develop the self-esteem to refuse the destructive influences of gangs.

The ravages of gang activities in our communities displease God. But so does the complacency of Christians who will not become involved to make things better. As we encourage involvement, however, we must recognize that this ministry, without good judgment and proper preparation, can be physically dangerous. Others in the community also care and want to make a difference. By seeking out these people and allowing God to draw us together in a united effort, God's power will overcome the evil in our midst.

SEEKING SOLUTIONS

Ministry Models

Just as gangs are spreading across our nation, community organizations and individuals are taking responsive actions. Many young people find alternatives to gangs through caring ministries that offer them what they seek. Most of these programs are preventive, giving young people a new vision of themselves as valued and having a future.

One such model is the Christian Activity Center in East St. Louis, Illinois. The center is located next to a housing project in a neighborhood with high unemployment and a high rate of school dropouts. The community has a long history of gangs, and many of the young people who attend center programs have older relatives who are in gangs. Center director Chet Cantrell knew that, without intervention and positive alternatives, the future for these children and youth would certainly involve gangs. He began developing programs that would meet some of their needs and take them off the streets. Over 100 young people attend the center each weekday afternoon for tutoring programs to help with homework. Because these children often do not receive affirmation at home for their academic achievements, Chet began having parties for those with good grades. After several years, he saw some of the first young people related to this program go to college. These and other activities provide opportunities for the young people to learn more about Jesus Christ and many decide to become Christians. An evening discipleship class helps young men grow in their Christian faith and in their leadership skills. They become new creations in Christ and new role models for the younger children in the neighborhood. The neighborhood still has gangs, but it also has high school graduates and children who see their value in God's sight through the eyes of people who offer them positive options for their future.

Another model comes from East Baptist Church in Philadelphia. Their ministry is known as the CAVE—the Center Against Violence Everywhere. The CAVE is a recreation center that provides alternatives to street corner and gang activity. It also offers Bible studies and discussion groups that address issues related to violence and youth development. Pastor Michael Pierce describes the community as "inner-city, approximately 60 percent public aid and 30 percent working people." The neighborhood is predominately Anglo, surrounded by increasingly integrated neighborhoods. Much of the area's gang activity is racially motivated. The CAVE program began when the pastor met with youth in the church to discuss why there was such a turnover in attendance. The youth suggested the idea of offering recreational activities to attract neighborhood youth. They even laid claim to a basement area in the church that had been used for storage. These youth, along with a Boy Scout in the church who needed a project, cleared and renovated the space. They raised money for equipment by placing "Can the Violence" donation cans in local businesses. Backed by local businesses and law enforcement, the program blossomed. The police even donated arcade games and a pool table confiscated from a crack house. Program volunteers maintain a tough stance against weapons, drugs, and fighting in the CAVE to make it safe for everyone. While the program encounters struggles, those associated with it know that the stakes are high. Gangs recruit children at increasingly younger ages. One of the newer gangs targets boys between the ages of 8–12.

High school drama teacher Doris Nash probably never initially intended to become involved in a gang-prevention ministry. Several years ago, her pastor at Bountiful Baptist Church in Little Rock, Arkansas, encouraged her to attend a meeting about a new apartment ministry. Soon Doris found herself the ministry's director. Under the primary sponsorship of Immanuel Baptist Church, the Pines Apartment Ministry provides food, clothing, Bible studies, and support for families in crisis. At about this same time, Doris began to notice graffiti at her school and an increase in the number of fights. Some of her students felt pressured to join gangs. After learning more about gangs, Doris began to look for new ways to work with students and involve others in working with small groups of those at risk. As their associations with these students grew, they discovered other needs they could meet, such as providing clothing and tutoring. Immanuel Baptist Church began offering basketball tournaments several times a year. Doris's involvement with the apartment ministry never had the primary goal of reducing gang influence, but it indirectly led her to this end. Gangs are less visible at Central High now. By becoming aware of needs and seeking to meet them, Doris and others were able to stand in the gap and give young people a rope to hold onto until other ministries developed.

In 1972, the Roman Catholic Church assigned Brother Modesto Leon to the Church of Our Lady of La Soledad in East Los Angeles. Alarmed by the number of funerals for young boys killed in gang initiations (three in a single month), he was burdened to do something. In one of his first moves, he brought together mothers of children killed in gang activities. Sometimes these were mothers of rival gang members; all were aggrieved and did not want to lose any more children. With a building from an elementary school, teachers from Catholic orders, and tutors from Cal State, Brother Modesto also started an alternative school for gang members who had dropped out. The school had one other thing: Concerned Mothers, by then a formal group. These mothers provided relay patrols to protect the students to and from school. Presently,

Concerned Mothers provides parental support that helps others recognize signs of beginning gang involvement. They also help teenaged mothers learn basic parenting skills. They continue to patrol streets and confront gang members. The Los Angeles Interagency Gang Task Force called Concerned Mothers "among the most effective antigang influences in Los Angeles." Brother Modesto was a catalyst in bringing together schools, parents, law enforcement officers, and the church to work together in attacking the problem of gangs in their neighborhood. He models for us one of the most important elements for effectively combating gangs: networking.

Some Underlying Principles

In each of the situations that serve as a ministry model for us, the church was either the primary ministry agent or a vital factor in the success of the ministry. The Christian church has a key role in diminishing the lure of gangs, a role that nothing else in the community can fill. Churches and communities take the first step toward combating gangs when they acknowledge that there is a problem. Churches that consider a ministry to gangs generally do so because something has happened to bring gang existence to their attention. Graffiti on the church walls, youth congregating in the church parking lot, a newspaper article—any of these can be the catalyst for a church's involvement. Individuals and churches that want to address problems resulting from gangs should verbalize the indicators they observe to help discover the nature and extent of the problem.

Next, learn as much as possible about the gang situation in your community. Each community is unique. Even gangs that have the same or similar names manifest themselves differently in different locations. Dress, hand signs, and graffiti that identify gangs are all unique to the community. To learn about gangs in your area, contact agencies within the community such as the local police, schools, youth organizations, the parks and recreation department, housing authorities, and apartment managers. Many cities have a gang task force that can provide information and can even lead an awareness conference for your church. As you gather information, seek answers to questions such as:

• How extensive is the gang problem in this community?
• Are there currently any programs that deal specifically with gangs?
• Who are the people most knowledgeable on this issue?
• What unmet needs in this community relate to youth?
• What do you feel a church or group of churches can do to help meet those needs?
• What resources and funds are available to meet those needs?

By gathering this information, you will begin to cultivate relationships with people and agencies with whom you will eventually work. A gang problem is a community problem and is most effectively overcome when everyone in the community cooperates. This is not a task the church should undertake in isolation.

When your church is committed to addressing the problem of gangs, decide which ministry you will undertake. Share the information with your church. Enlist members to pray for the ministry and be involved in its implementation. Ministry approaches fall into three categories: *awareness, prevention,* and *intervention.*

Awareness deals with educating adults, youth, and/or children about the nature, dangers, and extent of gangs in your community. One example of this approach is an awareness conference. Youth workers, parents, teenagers, and volunteers working with at-risk youth can all benefit from such a conference. You may identify future volunteers for other ministries from the people who attend.
Prevention involves programs and relationships that provide young people with alternatives to gang participation. Many traditional church ministries are preventive. Tutoring, afterschool clubs, recreation, and mentoring

programs provide young people with positive adult relationships and role models that build self-esteem and a
sense of belonging. These programs are more effective
deterrents if the leaders are knowledgeable about gangs
and discourage gang involvement.

Intervention provides support, alternatives, and resources for
young people involved in (but not yet hard-core
members of) gangs to enable them to leave gang life.
Intervention usually targets fringe members and wanna-
bes. Effective programs are those which are creative and
relevant to the lives of those you target. Intervention
most often occurs when someone develops a relationship
with an individual young person. Intervention may also
take the form of action through which the community
takes a stand against gangs. Community marches and
graffiti abatement programs are examples of intervention
ministries. Whichever ministry approach you choose, be
sure that everyone involved in the ministry is properly
oriented and prepared. Lack of preparation can lead not
only to ineffective results but also can place volunteers in
danger. Good preparation includes:

•Learning as much as you can about gangs in general and the
gangs in your community in particular.
•Sharing information about the extent of gang activity in
your community, its location, contributing factors, and
resulting problems.
•Reviewing what is being done and needs that still exist.
•Developing realistic expectations about a ministry to address
gangs.
•Arranging for an orientation if you are not a resident of the
community. Understand the community, its history,
character, and dangers.

A goal of any Christian ministry is to share our faith in
Christ in a meaningful way. We want others to know the saving grace of Jesus Christ and the transforming power of the
Holy Spirit. This ministry, like any other that is a valid ministry of Christ and His church, will grow from His love

within us. Christians want everyone to know Christ's love in a personal way.

At times, your ministry with people affected by gangs may test the limits of that love. You may struggle to remember that no one is beyond the reach of Christ's forgiveness and redemption. The young people with whom you minister may have developed a tough facade in order to survive. Look beneath the surface and ask God to help you see each person as He sees them.

You do not have to be a pushover to show that you care. All young people listen more receptively to adults they respect. Respect is a very important concept for gang-related youth. In order for them to hear and believe us, we must be "wise as serpents" at all times and gentle as lambs occasionally.

Get to know individuals and their families, if possible. Some people with whom you minister have had no exposure to the church or will come from a non-Christian background. Others have known the church only as an irrelevant or ineffectual institution and have formed their concepts of God accordingly. Still others may have some roots in the church but may have strayed or have never made a personal commitment to Christ. Never assume anything. But do take the time to learn about the spiritual life of those to whom you minister.

Start with each person where he or she is. Your witness will begin with your attitudes and actions. Allow people to know and trust you. Most of those with whom you work have pasts filled with betrayals. Be sensitive to God's leadership and timing, allowing Him to make your verbal witness a natural part of the relationship and situation. While you may have opportunities in preventive ministries to talk with a group, that which is most effective happens on an individual basis when a young person is not concerned with presenting a certain image to peers.

Avoid using theological terms that have no meaning to the person with whom you are talking. Train yourself to look for relevant ways to relate Christ and the Scriptures to their lives. Jesus is our model in this, as He frequently used parables and illustrations of people's life situations to relate spiritual truth.

When using Scripture, use a contemporary translation, and keep short, appropriate Scripture leaflets available.

Cultivate the ability to share in simple, everyday language not only your conversion experience but also how God relates to your daily life. Your sincerity will come through even when your words are inadequate.

Allow for questions as you talk. Do not feel you must have all the answers. Allow time for genuine understanding. You may introduce many new ideas that will require some time to process. Once the person does understand, make it clear that he or she is responsible for making his or her own decision in response to God and Christ.

Pray constantly for God to work in your own heart and in the hearts of those with whom you minister. Then you and they will be prepared for the teachable moments when Christ's good news is communicated.

Chapter Seven

CULTIVATE DOMESTIC HARMONY

By Fran Porter

Ester Atkins and Shawna Gale Brown lived short lives in which the people they trusted most, in the end, were the ones they should have trusted least." Thus begins an article in the Waco *Tribune-Herald*, accompanied by this byline: "Witness Beyond Death." Atkins was killed in her home by her boyfriend. Brown was shot and killed by her ex-husband as she left her place of employment.[1] The article also gave an account of a demonstration at the Texas Capitol remembering 150 Texas women who, in just one year, had been slain by their husbands and boyfriends. Volunteers erected life-size, cutout silhouettes, one for each of the victims. More than 500 people participated in the accompanying rally.

Deaths like Ester's and Shawna's are tragic, even shocking, but not unusual. "Spouse abuse leads to almost 100,000 days of hospitalization, 30,000 emergency room visits, and 40,000 trips to the doctor each year."[2] Vast numbers of women experience violence and abuse. During both 1992 and 1993, women were the victims of more than 4.5 million violent crimes, including approximately 500,000 rapes or other sexual assaults. In 29 percent of the violent crimes against women by lone offenders the perpetrators were intimates— husbands, former husbands, boyfriends, or former boyfriends.[3] And women are not the sole victims of family violence. A *Washington Times* article noted one study that reported 124 assaults by wives against their husbands per 1,000 married couples.[4]

We live in a violent environment. We hear "kill him" at sporting events. We laugh at cartoons in which people and animals are hit, punched, and pummeled with fists and weapons. When we are faced with conflict, our philosophy often seems to be "Get the other guy before he gets you." Power and control appear to be characteristics that are desired over reconciliation and meekness.

Domestic violence has no favorites. Spousal abuse occurs in big cities and rural communities; it happens to women of faith in our churches and to women with no religious affiliation; it affects young women and older women. It does not distinguish between educated women or women with little schooling. Abuse affects women who are conciliatory and women who are disagreeable. Spousal abuse is widespread and nondiscriminatory—it is an equal opportunity vice!

Unfortunately, the effects of spousal abuse are not limited to the immediate victims. Violence creates a cycle that perpetuates violence, and children as well as other family members may become victims of abusive treatment. Not only are between 2 and 4 million women abused each year, but the American Medical Association cites that domestic violence kills 2,000 to 4,000 women annually.[5] The estimate of child abuse cases is conservatively placed at more than 1 million a year. Five percent of dependent elderly Americans are physically abused in their own homes, usually by a relative. Neglect of the elderly is more widespread than physical abuse.

With the exception of the police forces and the military services, the family unit is the most violent social group in our nation.

The Family Abuse Center of Waco, Texas, has a motto: Love doesn't have to hurt! Sounds pretty good, but to the women who have suffered pain, injury, and humiliation at the hands of an abuser, there is often little comfort in words. Even the abused women themselves wonder what they did wrong. What could they have done differently?

BIBLICAL FOUNDATIONS

Christian women, both those abused and those who are safely cherished and loved, have God-directed beginnings:

> "Then God said, 'Let us make man in our image, in our likeness. . . . So God created man in his own image, in the image of God he created him, male and female he created them" (Gen. 1:26–27).

> "What is man that you are mindful of him, the son of man that you care for him? You made him a little lower than the angels; you crowned him with glory and honor and put everything under his feet" (Heb. 2:6*b*, 7).

> "Don't you know that you yourselves are God's temple and that God's Spirit lives in you? If anyone destroys God's temple, God will destroy him; for God's temple is sacred, and you are that temple" (1 Cor. 3:16–17).

As individuals created in God's very own image, women are creatures of worth and value, carefully made to reflect God's grace and love. "For you created my inmost being; you knit me together in my mother's womb" (Psalm 139:13). Unfortunately, many do not yet know this.

Human beings, male and female, are beautiful, wondrous creations. Violence should never have a part in the way we care for God's creation. When a woman recognizes her worth but feels cut off from her source of help and strength, there is ample evidence that God cares for His own and hears her cries:

> "Be strong and courageous. Do not be afraid or terrified because of them, for the Lord your God goes with you; he will never leave you nor forsake you" (Deut. 31:6).

> "The Lord is my helper; I will not be afraid. What can man do to me?" (Heb. 13:6*b*).

Psalm 27 also speaks to us of our relationship to God. He is our light, our salvation, our stronghold, our protector. This same Psalm exhorts us to learn the ways of the Lord and encourages us to be strong and courageous. Psalm 46:1–3 reminds us that God is our strength and refuge, a proven help in times of trouble. The last verses of that Psalm encourage us to be still and remember that the God of Jacob is our refuge. Perhaps one of the best-known sources of hope, strength, and encouragement is the familiar passage of Psalm 23, especially the fourth verse: "Even though I walk through the valley of the shadow of death, I will fear no evil, for you are with me; your rod and your staff, they comfort me."

SEEKING SOLUTIONS

Ministry Models

Until 1987, when I first began working to develop a program of transitional housing for victims of domestic violence, I had no real understanding of spousal abuse. I was overwhelmed by the variety of services women need as they try to escape a violent, abusive relationship: safe housing, self-esteem counseling, parenting techniques, daily living skills, assistance with governmental services (such as Medicaid and food stamps), transportation, and education. Most of the women my agency served came from the lower end of the socioeconomic scale because they had no place else to turn. I quickly learned that churches, synagogues, professional groups, service organizations, and caring individuals could and should make a vast difference. The needs were so many; there had to be a way to utilize the skills and abilities of interested groups and individuals.

Individuals, civic clubs, and service organizations have helped abused women find healing and encouragement by:

Educating themselves. It is imperative that those who want to help know all they can about domestic violence—

causes, statistics, needs, resources, preventions, and opportunities for service in their area.

Identifying helping agencies. It is also essential that they become familiar with the staffs of emergency shelters, transitional housing programs, Departments of Human Resources, public schools, social service agencies, adult and child protective services, legal aide, and police departments in their communities.

Being advocates for peace, justice, and fair treatment for all people.

Being listening allies.

Specifically, individuals in Waco, Texas, have volunteered in multiple ways. Many individuals go through training at the local emergency shelter to become shelter volunteers. Training provides volunteers with skills to answer the phone on a crisis line, to be sensitive listeners to shelter residents, and to work with children living at the shelter. Other individuals collect personal items (shampoo, bath soap, toothpaste, toothbrushes, personal hygiene products, combs, brushes, and hand lotion) to give to a shelter. None of these items may be purchased with a food stamp card. Some individuals provide transportation from the shelter to the courthouse, to a doctor's appointment, or to an educational facility or church where people can obtain a Graduate Equivalency Diploma. Since many abused women have been forced to abandon their homes with only what they could wear or carry, clothing is a need. Many individuals donate clean, usable clothes. Check with your local emergency shelter or long-term housing agency to know ways individuals can be personally involved.

Civic groups and service organizations usually have budgeted resources and can provide help with expenses. Congregations and other groups can provide an outing for several abused women and their children—a picnic, a trip to the zoo, a Christmas party with gifts for the women and children, a trip to the public library. Some groups have volunteered to do manual labor at a facility—paint, clean, dig a flower bed, or sort through contributions. Other groups keep the facility stocked with washcloths, bandages, canned meats, kitchen utensils for a newly arriving family or a departing family moving into independent housing, school supplies, and paper supplies.

The list of ways an organization can help is endless and is generally limited only by the creativity of those involved. Lake Shore Baptist Church in Waco, Texas, involves children in the ministry to victims of domestic violence. In their summer programs for children, Helping Hands and Bridge Builders, the children bring useful items to give to the emergency shelter or to the transitional housing program. They contribute items such as bath soap, washcloths, paper towels, boxes of crayons, notebook paper, tennis shoes, and children's books. The children then go with their sponsors to the designated facility to deliver the gifts. While at the helping agency, the children perform a ministry such as planting flowers or washing windows. Then they have a picnic on the grounds of the shelter. Often, the director of the shelter speaks to the children, explaining why families are there and how the children's presence is helpful. Hands-on ministries are wonderful teaching opportunities.

A group of women working in insurance companies made a commitment to provide school supplies for the local emergency shelter. This is a continuous project because the children who receive the supplies move out and take some of the supplies with them. Other children come to the shelter and the cycle of need begins again. This kind of project is easy and appropriate for a civic or service group. It does not require a great deal of time, but provides needed supplies. The women are constantly reminded of the magnitude of the problem of abuse and the continuous needs.

One year, when the Girls in Action of Texas attended a statewide event in Waco, they brought with them washcloths, cotton balls, and boxes of bandages. This project taught awareness and the idea that small items are valuable and useful.

Some Underlying Principles

A young mother in her 30s never had the opportunity to go to college or be trained for a professional vocation. She married young and had two children very quickly. When the children were 10 and 12, the mother began a nursing program at the local community college. She loved learning. She was an A student. Her professors were as proud of her academic accomplishments as she was.

This young family belonged to a Baptist church in their neighborhood. In fact, they shared the fence in back of their yard with one of the church's staff members. Sunday School, children's choir, and missions programs were a part of the family's week-to-week lives. Both children were also on a community baseball team.

The father traveled and was away frequently. When he was in town, he took no part in family church activities. He was not at all comfortable with his wife going to school. He became verbally and emotionally abusive. As is typical, the abuse became more frequent and more severe, escalating to physical abuse.

At the community college, the young woman's grades began to slip. She missed some classes. A sensitive professor inquired, asking if anything was wrong. Always, the woman responded negatively: "Nothing is wrong. I just have a lot on my mind. I am extremely busy." This behavior proceeded for several days and into weeks. Still, the woman said nothing. Her grades continued to slide downward.

The professor could take it no longer and called the woman to her office almost demanding to know what was going on. What was causing a bright nursing student to begin making such low grades? In relief and gratitude, the student began to pour out her heart and problems. She related a story of increasing physical abuse. Her husband had literally moved her and the children out of the house, leaving furniture and personal belongings in the yard.

Devastated, without any family in the community, the woman did not know what to do. In desperation, she rescued a few clothes and personal items for herself and the children; stuck some pillows and covers in the back of her vehicle, picked up the children from ball practice, and began to drive around. She had little cash in her purse. That night, she drove to a self-storage facility with a bright security light. She and the children slept in the car.

The next day, this courageous woman took college tuition money she had saved for the next semester and bought a membership in the YMCA. That way, she and the children could go there in the afternoons and have a quiet place to play and study. They could take showers and wash their hair. At bedtime, they piled back into the car, drove to the security light at the storage facility, and slept—two children and an adult—praying they would be safe until morning. This had been going on for four weeks when the professor pried the information from the student.

During these weeks, the children had missed children's choir at church. They had not gone to any missions meetings and had not been in Sunday School. They did continue school and baseball practice. Never in all this time did anyone from the church try to make contact with the family. Even though church friends were at the ball practices and dropped their children off at the same school, no one inquired or told the mother or children they had missed them at church.

What does this story say about us, people of the church? It is imperative that we develop an awareness and sensitivity to the people around us. It is equally imperative that we act spontaneously and show genuine concern when something appears to be amiss with our neighbors and friends. To act with sensitivity and show love means that we become Christlike. And to be Christlike, we must understand the calling to salvation and service.

I was an adult woman, married with children before I truly became aware that spousal abuse existed. Not only does it exist, it is pervasive. In the same ways that we become knowledgeable about issues of race, the problems at our children's schools, or ministry needs within our families of faith, we must become sensitive and knowledgeable about the issues of domestic violence.

What can you, as an individual, do to help alleviate the problem of spousal abuse?

•Understand your calling to salvation and ministry. Read the Scriptures for knowledge and understanding. Read anew about the lifestyle and practices of Jesus. He targeted the powerless and found opportunities to build relationships with them. He ministered to their needs and demonstrated love, compassion, and nonjudgment. Stay spiritually alert through prayer, meditation, and study of the Scriptures.

•Develop a relationship with community agencies that serve victims of spousal violence. Learn of the causes, needs, and services provided. Be an advocate in your community.

•Work for peace: "God blesses those people who make peace. They will be called his children!" (Matt. 5:9 CEV). Practice peace in your own life—in your home, workplace, church, and community. Support and promote organizations and programs that work for peace (such as Baptist Peace Fellowship of North America, Witness for Peace, and others.)

•Minister from your church base. As you develop ministries, you can share reports, testimonies, and prayer requests on a periodic basis with your church family through missions groups, Sunday School classes, prayer meetings, and your church newsletter.

Spousal abuse is a shameful reality in our society. It is unlawful, sinful, and dehumanizing. God wants to bring healing, and He has chosen us to be instruments of His peace.

Chapter Eight

RESPECT YOUR ELDERS

By Bill Howse

The issue of elder abuse began to prick America's conscience during the late 1970s. It was then that a group of Boston researchers used a federal grant to test their hypothesis related to abuse and the elderly. They reasoned something akin to child abuse was affecting the growing number of older adults in this country.[1]

Not only did their studies reveal abuse among the elderly, they also set off a chain reaction. First, there was a series of articles on their findings. Then, in 1981, the late Representative Claude Pepper put congressional hearings in motion. These hearings turned into investigations that uncovered emotional stories of abuse and neglect of the American aged.[2] A flurry of legislative initiatives followed the hearings, establishing identification, intervention, and resolution processes for elder abuse similar to those already in place for child abuse.[3]

The National Center on Elder Abuse reported 241,000 incidents of domestic abuse cases in 1994. Elder abuse takes many forms but is generally categorized as *physical, psychological, neglect,* and *financial.*

Physical abuse includes slapping, hitting with extreme force, bruising, pushing, the use of various restraining devices, burning, and other actions that inflict injury.

Psychological abuse, on the other hand, includes such demeaning behavior as threats, insults, name-calling, and treating the older person as a child. Psychological or emotional abuse results in feelings of mental anguish and loss of self-esteem on the part of the older person.

Neglect is perhaps the most common type of abuse against the elderly and can cover a wide range of behaviors. Not providing appropriate food or health care services, withholding such necessities as hearing aids and eyeglasses, leaving the older person abandoned or isolated for long periods of time, or even failing to give important news or information all constitute neglect. This type of neglect may be deliberate, causing stress for the older person. Or it may be unintentional due to inadequate skills, knowledge, or understanding on the part of the caregiver.

Financial abuse includes a range of illegal or unethical actions such as taking a Social Security check without proper authorization, coercing an older person to sign over property or other assets, and denying the right to make financial decisions.

Is elder abuse a real problem in American society? Research suggests not only that it is but also that it could get worse, primarily because of the growing numbers of aging persons in our society. "One of the sad realities of caring for old people is it can seem like it's going to go on forever. . . . With children, you know they're going to grow up, but with an old person some begin to feel that the only way to deal with this daily is to look forward to their death."[4]

Studies suggest that family members, more specifically adult children, are the most frequent abusers of older adults. There are no clear reasons why younger family members turn on older family members. Generally, abuse occurs when families feel pressured by numerous economic, social, and psychological forces. People who mistreat the elderly frequently have personal problems such as alcohol or drug addiction, financial pressures, or a history of mental or emotional disorders. "The typical victim of elder abuse is a white woman in her 70s. But there is also no evidence a woman is necessarily safer if she is black, Asian, Hispanic or American Indian."[5] The typical abuser is an "adult child or someone else close to the victim, for instance a caretaker, an accountant, a preacher."[6]

BIBLICAL FOUNDATIONS

Interestingly, the Bible does not specifically address elder abuse. However, abuse is mentioned three times in the Bible, all in the Old Testament. Several biblical concepts are applicable to the issue of elder abuse.

Beginning with the Book of Genesis, the Bible makes numerous references to age. Age is, in fact, an important theme in Genesis, which describes a man's age at the time of marriage, fathering his first child, and death. Genesis clearly views longevity positively. For example, Methuselah's 969 years (Gen. 5:27) staggers our imagination, especially when we think of 100 years being a long life today. Adam lived 930 years (Gen. 5:5) and Enos 905 years (Gen. 5:11). Enoch walked with God for 300 years (Gen. 5:22). Lamech lived 777 years (Gen. 5:31) and Noah 950 years (Gen. 9:29).

The fifth commandment, found in Exodus 20:12, is clearly an admonition to have respect for parents, reminding us to "honor your father and mother." Exodus also frequently mentions the phrase "elders of Israel." These persons were a respected part of the early communities and synagogues. A number of them were likely older and possessed great knowledge and wisdom and therefore had the respect of others.

The Book of Proverbs develops the notion of wisdom. While wisdom is not necessarily a part of aging alone, the Bible encourages us both to seek it and to revere it.

New Testament accounts in the gospels as well as in Acts reveal some important considerations about the subject of aging. One is related to service. Matthew 25:35 reminds us about the importance of ministering to persons in need. Christ's example encourages us to do things for others, such as providing caregiving ministries to an elderly family member or friend.

Love is, of course, an underlying theme throughout the New Testament. First Corinthians 13 describes Godlike love for us; the implication is obvious for those with responsibilities for elderly persons. Another New Testament theme involves respect for parents. Ephesians 6:1–3 tells us, "Children, obey your parents in the Lord, for this is right.

'Honor your father and mother'—which is the first commandment with a promise—'that it may go well with you and that you may enjoy long life on earth.'" These passages remind us to view our parents with respect, honor, and love.

> Aging should be on the side of maturity, wisdom, goodness and fulfillment. Sometimes it is and sometimes it is not. The kings Saul and Solomon got worse with age; Jacob and Paul got better.[7]

SEEKING SOLUTIONS

The following suggestions illustrate ways you can address elder abuse in your church and community. Let these be a guide as you develop solutions to needs you discover.

•Design a series of classes on the subject of abuse for your church family. Use these classes to identify and encourage healthy lifestyles among members of all ages, as well as educate people about types of abusive behaviors; how to avoid abusive behavior; and some alternative ways to deal with conflict, frustration, and anger. Both intergenerational and age-defined classes can be effective, and such classes are appropriate any time during the year.
•Invite as a guest speaker a social worker from a residential care facility, the local Council on Aging or Area Agency on Aging, or a state agency that deals with abuse. This individual can also offer training to church visitation committees, the pastor, other church staff members, deacons, elders, and other church leaders. Such training can help them recognize signs of abuse, educate them concerning state laws covering abuse, and suggest steps to take should they discover instances of elder abuse. Consider both a onetime training event and ongoing training over a longer period of time, depending upon your needs. A social worker or speaker in this area will also be a helpful and informative resource for older adults in the church.

•Develop a support group for elder caregivers in your church and community. Such a group can provide them a place to discuss common concerns in a confidential setting and can assure them that that they are not alone in the situations they encounter.

•Establish a respite care ministry using volunteers. This will allow elder caregivers some relief and time away from their responsibilities on a regular basis. If community programs of respite care already exist, enlist volunteers to support and enhance these programs.

•Provide an information and referral service through your church. Collect and keep a supply of pamphlets, brochures, and other information pieces from public service agencies such as the local Council on Aging or Area Agency on Aging, dealing with family violence, early detection, intervention, and identifying available services. Make this information service available not only to church members but also to members of your neighborhood and community.

•Enlist an attorney to lead a meeting for members of your church and community and to discuss the legal channels available for abused adults.

•Develop a voluntary assistance program in your church to provide services for older adults, such as minor home repairs and transportation to grocery stores, doctors' offices, and banks. Not only do these types of services allow regular visitation and contact with older adults and meet real needs, they also can allow for early detection of abuse and appropriate intervention.

The issue of elder abuse is complex and difficult and calls for a studied response from Christians. It affects families in various ways. The abused are afraid to report abuse for fear of retaliation. Those who discover abuse or to whom abuse is reported must consider and respect the elderly person's right to privacy. At the same time, they must take appropriate action so that the abuse stops. A Christian response involves both prevention and intervention. We have a responsibility to get as much correct information as possible. One of the best ways to do this is to contact a local or state government office that deals with abuse of the elderly. Armed with this information, look for ways to be involved with others in your area. Consider becoming an advocate for abused and neglected elderly in your community. Just as you pray for peace in the world and in your community, pray that families will cultivate respect for their oldest members, thereby ending acts of abuse and neglect against them.

Suggestions for Families

These simple suggestions can help families avoid problem situations that might escalate to abuse.

•Keep in touch with older family members or other elderly persons on a regular basis. This will increase your awareness of the possibility of abuse from outside sources.

•When possible, take advantage of adult day care, home health aides, recreation programs, training for caregivers, and transportation assistance. These lessen the stress factors caregivers experience and therefore can decrease the likelihood of abuse.

•Plan for emergencies, and involve the older person in this process. Discuss what to do about bank accounts, the will, contents of safe-deposit boxes, debts, and insurance policies. Keep this information confidential. Family members who maintain regular contact with the senior adult can more easily recognize whether this information has been given to someone who wants to take advantage of the situation.

•If you are a caregiver, schedule regular personal breaks, and ask for help from family or friends. Seek relief before you reach the breaking point. If you are a volunteer caregiver, don't consider yourself a failure if a particular helping situation doesn't work out.

Responsibilities of Older Persons

Older adults may find the following suggestions helpful in avoiding potentially abusive situations:

•Plan for a possible disability by completing an advance medical directive and arranging for durable power of attorney. Work out the details with appropriate family members or a close friend.

•Enlarge your circle of friends. Remain sociable and stay active in your community and church for as long as possible. This will enable friends to become aware of any possible changes in your routines and habits. Ask friends to visit you at home. This helps them to observe your well-being and can help when family members do not live close by.

•Familiarize yourself with community resources that help older people remain independent.

•Never share a household with anyone who has a history of violent behavior or substance abuse or with anyone you do not already know. Also avoid moving in with a child or relative if the relationship is already strained or troubled.

•Do not hesitate to ask for assistance from a lawyer, physician, family member, or trusted friend. Getting questions answered in a timely manner can keep problems from arising.

•Never give control of your money to someone in exchange for favors without a trusted friend as a witness. Elderly people are the targets of many scams. Do not sign documents unless someone you trust has reviewed them.

•Have a telephone so that you can have immediate contact with others. Discuss your concerns with the postal authorities if you think your mail is being tampered with or intercepted.

•Keep all of your belongings in order. Do not advertise your personal matters. Avoid leaving your valuables lying about your home.

•Arrange for your Social Security check to be deposited directly to your bank account.

•Keep regular dental, barber, hairdresser, and other appointments. These professionals can attest to your competence and well-being.

•One of the easiest and best ways to decrease the potential for abuse is to participate in a Neighborhood Watch program. If one is not available in your area, work with others to begin such a program. Some of these programs also include abuse prevention training.

Chapter Nine

BUILD BRIDGES OF LOVE

By Alpha Goombi

Mario is angry. He and his brother, a gentle young man, often cannot walk down the streets of their Omaha neighborhood without being stopped and questioned by local police. Women who pass Mario and his friends on the sidewalk often clutch their purses more tightly. Sometimes they even cross the street to avoid close contact. Mario's offense? He is African-American.

As children growing up in rural Oklahoma, my sisters and I could not go into the local dime store in our hometown without the store clerk following us and watching our every move. We faced verbal taunting and racial prejudice in school. Our offense? We are Native American Indians.

Recently our van was stolen from our Baptist center parking lot. The van is vital to our ministry because most of the people who attend worship services and other activities there do not have transportation. The center is located in an inner-city Omaha neighborhood that is in racial transition. The area used to be home primarily to Italian immigrants. Now it is a melting pot of African Americans, Anglos, Native Americans, Hispanics, the elderly, internationals, and immigrants from Mexico, Central America, and South America. Police found the van two days after its disappearance, burned and floating in a nearby lake. It was a total loss and an ugly act of violence.

Lee is trapped and confused. He arrived in America with his family from East Asia, filled with dreams for a better life.

73

Things have been anything but easy. The family has faced prejudice, hatred, and threats from those who view them as inferior and as competition for jobs. Lee's parents settled into low-paying jobs that call for skills well below what their education and experience could allow them. While they continue to seek more and better opportunities, Lee has seen them grow disillusioned and lose hope. Determined to climb to the top more quickly than his parents, Lee turned to crimes and gang life at the age of 16. His activities are illegal and often violent, but they result in more money than his parents ever dreamed of. In spite of the risks and danger to his personal safety, Lee sees no reason to leave the life that has brought him financial stability and a sense of belonging.

The stories of these individuals, snatched from the pages of real lives, are repeated across our nation. Almost one-fourth of America's 265 million people are members of a minority, racial, or ethnic group. By 2050, Anglos will represent only 53 percent of the total US population. Classifications of racial or ethnic origin, according to the Census Bureau, have divided the American population into five major ethnic groups: non-Hispanic White, Black, Asian/Pacific Islander, American Indian/Eskimo/Aleut, and Hispanic.[1] These classifications reveal sad statistics related to violence.

The Federal Bureau of Investigation reported 7,947 incidents of hate crime in the US in 1995, 61 percent of which were motivated by racial bias. These incidents involved more than 10,000 victims and over 8,000 known offenders. Intimidation was the single most frequently reported hate crime offense, accounting for 41 percent of the total. As in previous years, these hate crimes were most frequently directed at individuals, with the remaining incidents targeting, among other things, businesses and religious organizations.[2]

African-American males aged 16 to 19 have a violent crime victimization rate almost double the rate for white males and three times the rate for Anglo females in the same age range, according to the National Crime Victimization Survey (NCVS). The same survey found that certain population groups are more likely to be victimized and are more vulnerable to violence than those who do not belong to these groups. African American males aged 12 to 24 were almost 14 times as likely to be homicide victims than were members of the general population. According to the findings of the NCVS, certain contributing factors put minority groups at greater risk of becoming victims or perpetrators of violent crimes.[3] African Americans are more likely to be victims of aggravated assault than are Anglos, Asians, or Native Americans. The young, African Americans, and males are most vulnerable to violent crime. In addition, Hispanics are more likely to be victims of aggravated assault than non-Hispanics.[4]

Racial violence involves hostility toward people of a different race, skin color, religion, or national origin. It can happen anywhere. And regardless of where it happens, it affects the peace and security of the entire community. Sometimes racial violence is subtle, such as a hateful glare. Other times it is extreme, involving assault, other forms of physical violence, and damage to property and buildings. Much of the time, it falls somewhere in between intimidation through physical and verbal threats, insults, telling racial or ethnic jokes, racist graffiti, and hate propaganda. Regardless of its forms, the effects of racism and resulting violence are devastating. Even if they suffer no physical harm, victims of racial violence suffer emotionally and psychologically and may experience repeated nightmares; loss of sleep and appetite; loss of self-esteem; stress, depression, and anger; and fear of leaving the safety of home.[5]

BIBLICAL FOUNDATIONS

God's prophet Habakkuk was troubled by the violence of his day and questioned how God could use the wicked Babylonians as instruments to execute His judgment and purpose. Habakkuk and the people of Israel struggled with the apparent triumph of the wicked while the righteous suffered. Habakkuk's struggle was personally profound. Listen to Habakkuk's dialogue with God: "How long, O Lord, must I call for help, but you do not listen? Or cry out to you, 'Violence!' but you do not save? Why do you make me look at injustice? Why do you tolerate wrong? Destruction and violence are before me; there is strife, and conflict abounds. Therefore the law is paralyzed, and justice never prevails. The wicked hem in the righteous, so that justice is perverted" (Hab. 1:2–4).

Victims of violence today share Habakkuk's pleas. A mother does not intend for her child to become the victim or the perpetrator of a violent crime. Most parents have higher aspirations for their children than gang life. Living in a crime-riddled neighborhood is a fate most Christians neither expect nor experience, yet thousands of godly Christians find themselves in such circumstances. Voices today cry out for deliverance, just as Habakkuk did. God had an answer for Habakkuk's prayer, and God's promise is relevant today. God's answer is redemption. "For the earth will be filled with the knowledge of the glory of the Lord, as the waters cover the sea," God tells Habakkuk (Hab. 2:14).

Redemption, of course, comes through a personal relationship with God through Jesus Christ. Our challenge in eliminating racially motivated violence is to take God's redemption to high-risk areas. God promised Habakkuk a day when the gospel message would be known worldwide, God's evangelistic purpose realized. God will fulfill His promise as we work to fulfill the Great Commission, as stated by Jesus in Matthew 28:18–20. The power of Jesus Christ to save people from their sins and to change their lives from within offers true hope to individuals, communities, and nations trapped in the cycle of violence.

"If anyone says, 'I love God,' yet hates his brother, he is a liar. For anyone who does not love his brother, whom he has seen, cannot love God, whom he has not seen. And He has given us this command: Whoever loves God must also love his brother" (1 John 4:20–21). The Christian heart has no room for racial stereotypes. God calls Christians to action through divine love.

Excuses abound for not reaching out to people and places tormented by violence that is racially motivated. Safety is certainly an issue, and God expects us to exercise wisdom and good judgment as we go. But as surely as God calls us to go to victims of racial violence, areas plagued by racial violence, and perpetrators of racial violence, He will protect us as we minister. The cost is too great for us not to respond.

SEEKING SOLUTIONS

The factors which lead to racially motivated violence are complicated and numerous. There is no single solution. But by working to change behavioral, environmental, and societal influences that lead to this kind of violence, and by increasing and supporting those factors that help offset violence, Christians can help eliminate future violent acts. You may choose to begin in your own family. In fact, that's the most logical place to start.

•Begin or continue to teach children that God loves everyone equally, that God created different races and colors of people, and that His creation is purposeful and good. Encourage these attitudes in your own home, and incorporate them into your church's educational programs as well. Promote an attitude of inclusiveness, acceptance, and affirmation of all people.

•Broaden your personal circle of friends to include people of various races and ethnic groups. Include your children and other children you know in these relationships. Help children see the positive contributions people of all races and cultures have made to the fabric of American society.

•Celebrate a holiday with a family of a race or culture different from yours. Incorporate traditions from both cultures in the day's activities and meals.

•Monitor your attitudes constantly, and be purposefully sensitive to the attitudes of those around you. Do your part to combat ignorance and prejudice. Every time you hear a racial slur or derogatory comment, follow it with a positive example or story of someone of that race or ethnic group. Take a stand against prejudicial conversation and attitudes, and teach the children over whom you have influence to do the same.

•Educate yourself about different races and cultures. Avoid operating out of a vacuum of ignorance. Before you begin any ministry among or with people of other races and cultures, learn as much as you can from them and about them. But avoid stereotyping them and assuming that all people of a certain culture or race believe or behave in certain ways. The best way to learn about other races and cultures is to become friends with people who represent them.

•Help raise awareness in your church and community about contributions people of various races and cultures have made. Emphasize positive people, events, and circumstances. Rarely are these highlighted or reported as regularly as the negatives. Work to eliminate racial stereotypes.

•Encourage your church to join with churches composed of people from other races and cultures in worship, fellowship, and ministry opportunities. Talk with pastors about initiating contacts with leaders of these churches for such possibilities. Take the initiative! A unified effort by churches representing different races and ethnic groups will make a strong statement to the community.

•Stay informed about acts of racial violence perpetrated in your community. Follow cases carefully, and see them through to resolution. Become an advocate for victims' rights.

•Help combat racially motivated violence by working to eliminate some of the factors that contribute to it: ignorance, prejudice, poverty, low self-esteem, unequal educational opportunities, alcohol, and drug abuse. Volunteer in existing community programs targeting these problems, or begin new programs where you see the need.

•Volunteer in existing programs which help strengthen minority families: parenting classes, information and educational campaigns, parent partnerships and mentorships, family mediation groups, anger management and conflict resolution classes, and classes offering training in life and social skills.

•Volunteer in programs encouraging cross-cultural adult/youth mentorships.

•Work for better educational opportunities for all people. Education is a way out of poverty and an avenue toward a better life. It helps boost self-esteem and reduces hopelessness and frustration, which can lead to violence.

•Work for equitable school resources and facilities, and become an advocate for safety at all schools, not just the ones in your neighborhood.

•Promote, support, and find new avenues for educational scholarships for minorities.

•Encourage minority youth and young adults to consider ministry and missions careers, and help them get the financial support they need to achieve their goals.

•Help minority teenagers find and keep jobs. Provide classes that teach them skills for job interviews as well as skills for specific jobs. Enlist the support of local businesses in offering employment to teenagers who want and need to work.

•Work for tougher laws governing weapon purchase and possession.

•Become intentional about ministry with and among people of other races and cultures. Remember that you do not have all the answers, but your God does.

Chapter Ten

THE UNSPEAKABLE CRIME

By Lora Smith

When people hear the term *sexual abuse*, many immediately think of rape. Rape is a major sexual abuse present in epidemic proportions in the United States, but it is far from being the only type of sexual abuse. There are many types of sexual abuse, which include sexual harassment, verbal abuse, physical abuse or force, visual abuse, child sexual abuse, sexual exploitation, incest, rape, and ritualistic sexual abuse. According to the National Victim Center, 700,000 women are raped or sexually assaulted each year. Of these victims, 61 percent are younger than the age of 18. The American Academy of Pediatrics estimates that male victims represent about 5 percent of reported sexual assaults.[1]

Sexual abuse is sometimes perpetrated by a stranger, but more often the victim/survivor knows his or her attacker. Often the abuse starts long before the perpetrator actually crosses the physical boundaries of the victim.[2] When the abuse does occur, the victim is confused and has many feelings that are difficult to resolve. Those feelings may include anger, betrayal, sadness, confusion, shame, guilt, fear, and loneliness. These often keep the victim from getting the help that he or she needs.

In *Shelter from the Storm: Hope for Survivors of Sexual Abuse,* the authors suggest that there are four lies with which victims have to deal:[3]

• "It's my fault." The victim accepts responsibility for the assault.

- "I must be a terrible person for him or her to do this to me!" Once the first lie is accepted, this one usually falls in line. This is particularly true for children since they have difficulty accepting that adults do wrong things.
- "I wanted him or her to do this to me." Since the human body responds to sexual stimulation, the victim misinterprets natural bodily reactions for personal desires and traps the mind into guilt.
- "It didn't happen! I must have made it up." To deny the abuse makes its recognition even harder.

Recovering from sexual abuse is a complicated process since it is recovery from a betrayal that assaults the body, mind, and soul. It is extremely difficult for a victim to recover without help. Tendencies of victims/survivors of sexual abuse may include: headaches, sleeplessness, sexual difficulties leading to frigidity or promiscuity, low self-esteem, lack of healthy boundaries, rage, overreaction, addictions, spacing out, memory block, perfectionism, the need for achievement, repeatedly feeling betrayed, withdrawal, anxiety, repeated victimization, seductive behavior, anger, depression, codependency, and self-destructive behavior.[4] Because of these issues, any ministry dealing in sexual abuse should have access to a Christian counselor who specializes in sexual abuse.

BIBLICAL FOUNDATIONS

Read Psalm 55. The psalmist is obviously in great anguish in this passage, betrayed by someone close to him. In a relationship in which the writer expected to find nurture, care, intimacy, and safety, he found a betrayed trust, fear, and violence. He had little, if any, confidence in trusting others who might hurt him the same way. He could only find comfort with God. He calls out with a four-point plea to God in verses 1 and 2: "Listen to my prayer," "do not ignore my plea," "hear me," and "answer me." He cries out for help to the only One Who will never betray him.

In the same way, victims of sexual abuse don't know whom they can trust, or even if they can trust themselves. In verse 12, the writer says that he would have been better able to handle the assault if it had come from a stranger or enemy, not someone close to him. He knew how to deal with enemies, but not with a friend or brother. When someone close betrays us, the pain is deep. It causes victims to withdraw for self-protection and/or indecision. They go within themselves. David says that if he had wings he would just fly away, get away from it all, escape. Escape is only a fantasy; it provides a safety valve but doesn't satisfy our deepest needs in times of trouble. Ignoring sexual abuse and running away from it may be a temporary solution, but it will not resolve the deepest needs in the victim's life. Finally, David turns from flight to fight. He strikes out and wants vengeance.

Consistently he called out in prayer, morning and evening, asking for deliverance from his burdens. God doesn't always take away our pain and burdens. Sometimes He just gives us extra measures of grace to endure them. Paul tells us in Romans 8:26–28 that the Spirit helps us in our weakness, searching our heart and making intercession for us in accordance with God's will. When we seek God's will and His purpose, then all things, including intimate betrayals and sexual abuse, can ultimately work for our good. The psalmist's feelings were reactions to real life situations, just as the victims' feelings are natural for what they have endured. People must decide which problems they can solve and which they can't. God is trustworthy, and He is able to solve all the problems that we can't concerning both people and circumstance.

SEEKING SOLUTIONS

When you look at the depth of pain and hurt, it is easy to see why two forms of help are being offered to victims of sexual abuse: professional counseling and support groups. Those who have started support groups within the church without previous training in sexual abuse quickly found themselves in over their heads and bailing out. Ministry in this area shouldn't be considered without a significant support network for the ministry. Let me share a real life example:

Annemarie was about 30 years old when she signed up for my self-defense class at the state university. Of all the students in the class only she exhibited a real victim posture. About three weeks into the class Annemarie was more lethargic and looked more pathetic than before. After class I stopped her in the hallway and asked if everything was all right. She broke down sobbing and said there was no one she could trust—her whole life was falling apart. I took her to a quiet area, bought her something to eat, and then listened to her horrific story for the next 90 minutes. Her story was one of verbal, physical, and sexual abuse, even bodily mutilation. She and her husband both professed to be born-again Christians but had extremely twisted interpretations of the Bible and how its message was intended to be applied. Her life was in danger and she needed immediate help, but she didn't have the confidence or courage to do what was needed. I asked her to trust me and lean on my strength until she could stand on her own.

We went to the director of the program she was in, and again she told the gruesome story. The program director suggested that she needed to get downtown to the Witness-Victim program. I volunteered to take her downtown while the director called Witness-Victim to fill them in. Once downtown, Annemarie again told her story. Patrick and Carman at Witness-Victim deeply believed that if Annemarie's daughters, aged eight and ten, arrived home without their mother they would be brutally attacked. On behalf of the Witness-Victim people I immediately left with Annemarie to pick up the children at school. Witness-Victim called the school, a shelter, the police, and the county prosecutor.

Before we picked up the girls, I asked Annemarie what she was going to tell them. She had no idea, so I offered to talk to them on her behalf. I started to share with them that their daddy had hurt Mommy. He was very sick and needed help, and they needed to be safe. Kelly, the younger girl, interrupted me and started telling us all she had observed over the years of the 12-year brutal marriage. Annemarie was shocked. She didn't think the girls had seen anything. Over the next nine months, the husband was charged and sentenced. He is now serving a 15-year prison term. Annemarie started her own healing through individual counseling, support groups, job training, and a church's love and outreach to her and her children. The children were so psychologically traumatized that they were placed in court custody with a children's advocate until they could regain their emotional health. When I asked Annemarie to trust me on the first day, I told her it would take a lot of courage to regain her holistic health. It wouldn't be easy. But I also promised her she wouldn't have to do it alone.

Establish sexual abuse policies for your church/church ministries: One of the greatest litigation areas churches face today is sexual abuse within the church. Research state and local laws. Get information on preventing abuse and offer seminars in small groups or for the church. Work to establish church policies. Establish a screening process for church positions, especially those that deal with children.

Counseling: Churches need to know when they should refer people to professional counselors. Interview counselors in your area to identify whether or not they specifically deal with sexual abuse. Screen them for their belief systems since many non-Christian counselors may offer advice contrary to biblical teachings. Establish a referral system and share it with other churches. Newer areas of counseling include play and art therapy that help children express what has happened or is happening to them. Even individuals without degrees can learn much of what is happening to the child if they really pay attention to how the child expresses himself or herself. Take some classes in these areas and become more informed on how to interpret what children are trying to say. Be a child's advocate.

Support groups: Offer a support group for people who have been victimized by sexual abuse. Remember that men can be abused. It is not sound judgment to offer coed support groups in this ministry area. Though facilitators don't need to be trained experts in the area of sexual abuse, they should have a background of some type in the dynamics of sexual abuse.

Hot lines: Volunteer to work existent hot lines in your community, or consider starting one if one doesn't exist. RAINN and 9 to 5 are national numbers listed on page 164. See what might be located near you. Do your research and networking homework before you consider starting a new hot line. It takes dozens of trained volunteers to maintain an around-the-clock hot line. There may be a local coordinating agency in your community that can tell you what hot lines already exist.

Hospital advocates: When sexually abused victims are brought to the hospital for medical help they often feel "victimized" again by the medical staff and police who question them. A hospital advocate is usually connected with the local rape crisis center and can be called once the victim is brought to the emergency room. The advocate's job is to remind medical personnel and police officers that this is the victim, not the perpetrator. The victim has rights and needs some time to process what has happened. A hospital advocate also serves as a support system for the victim since he or she may be there before family or friends. Advocates are trained to explain to the victim why everything is being done and what will happen next.

Court advocacy: Many victims of sexual abuse eventually make it to the justice system, which is often scary and intimidating. Decisions are made without informing the victim or survivor. Court advocates can work with either the rape crisis center or the witness-victim program in your community. They both maintain volunteer work forces. Call to see how you can get involved.

Court watch: Only a percentage of those initially charged with sexual offenses are actually convicted. Of those charged and found guilty, only a percentage are incarcerated. Once they are sent to jail, they only serve about one-third of their sentences. As a ministry, individuals may write letters to the judge saying how important it is for the perpetrator to be held accountable and for victims to receive justice. Recruit individuals to attend the trials to let the judge know that the community is watching how he handles his responsibility.

Educational programming at school/church: Offer conferences and classes that deal with issues such as self-esteem, power and control, good and bad touching, forgiveness, proper boundaries, clarification of roles, accountability, and so forth. These classes should be started as early as possible so that children growing up in a sexually deviant family can begin relearning proper roles before they begin replicating their parents' behaviors.

Self-defense classes: Sexual abuse is about power and control. A good self-defense class can help victims and potential victims take back control and feel empowered. There are many kinds of martial arts. Most are sports-orientated. Seek out and screen a good martial arts instructor who has had some training and/or experience with victims of sexual abuse and is sensitive to the related issues. Though a onetime class can be offered, I suggest, based on my experience, that a course be held over a period of six to ten classes to allow participants to integrate the training fully.

Volunteer in a shelter: If there is a shelter for sexually abused people in your community, consider volunteering there. If not, create a coalition of people and/or churches to begin one. Make sure the shelter's location is kept confidential. Other shelters in town or your state can help you learn the basics for beginning a shelter in your community. There may be numerous legal considerations in this undertaking. Seek legal counsel to assist with incorporating boards and training.

Chapter Eleven

THROW DOWN THE STICKS AND STONES

By Trudy Johnson

Sticks and stones may break my bones but words will never hurt me. Children attempt to defuse the damage of harsh, condemning words by chanting this familiar refrain. We learn early in life that *words do hurt.* The sting of the damaging words lingers long after any chant we might offer in retort. And sometimes, unfortunately, occasional "sticks and stones" become a pattern of ongoing verbal abuse.

Verbal abuse consists of derogatory comments, insults, and constant put-downs.[1] It also includes threats of physical violence and violent verbal outbursts.[2] At the root of verbally abusive behavior lies anger, power, and control. Women and children are the primary victims of verbal abuse, and the results are always the same. Although verbal abuse leaves no outward marks, it can scar the psyche for a lifetime.

Part of creating a safer world involves recognizing verbal abuse, ministering to its victims, and dealing with its perpetrators. Verbal abuse damages the human spirit. Its victims often lack the necessary awareness, emotional strength, and knowledge to free themselves from it and the violent situations that sometimes follow. This chapter is a call to educate ourselves to recognize verbal abuse, to equip ourselves to care for its victims, and to evaluate persons and programs in our communities prepared to deal with the abuser.

Ugly, angry spoken words characterize verbal abuse in its most recognizable form. But it has a more covert side, too.

Indirect attacks can be covert. This kind of abuse has been described as *crazymaking*.[3] George R. Bach and Ronald M. Deutsch, in their book *Stop! You're Driving Me Crazy*, state:[4]

The following checklist is of value in teaching recognition of the crazymaking experience:

- Feeling temporarily thrown off balance and unable to right oneself.
- Feeling lost, not knowing where to turn.
- Being caught off guard.
- Feeling confused, disoriented.
- Feeling off balance, as if the rug had been pulled from under one's feet.
- Receiving double messages but being somehow unable or fearful to ask for clarification.
- Feeling generally "bugged" by the simple presence of a person.
- Discovering that one was mistaken in one's evaluation of where one stood.
- Feeling totally unprepared for a broken promise or unfulfilled expectation.
- Experiencing the shattering of an important "dream."
- Finding ill will where one had assumed good will.
- Feeling pushed around, not in control of one's own direction.
- Being unable to get off redundant spinning circles of thoughts.
- Finding what seemed clear becoming muddled.
- Having an uneasy, weird feeling of emptiness.
- Having a strong wish to get away, yet feeling unable to move, as if frozen.
- Feeling befuddled, not able to attack the problem.
- Feeling vaguely suspicious that something is wrong.
- Feeling that one's subjective world has become chaotic.

Victims of verbal abuse recognize these feelings and often accept them as normal because the effects of verbal abuse impair their perceptions. As difficult as it may be for someone who is not in an abusive relationship to understand, victims of verbal abuse learn to tolerate the abuse without even realizing it. Out of a lack of understanding of the motives of the abusers (often their mates), they "live on hope."[5]

Verbal abuse results not in bruises or broken bones but in bruised and broken spirits. Patricia Evans, in *The Verbally Abusive Relationship*, lists these primary consequences of verbal abuse in a victim:[6]

- A distrust of her spontaneity.
- A loss of enthusiasm.
- A prepared, on-guard state.
- An uncertainty about how she is coming across.
- A concern that something is wrong with her.
- An inclination to soul-searching and reviewing incidents with the hope of determining what went wrong.
- A loss of self-confidence.
- A growing self-doubt.
- An internalized "critical voice."
- A concern that she isn't happier and ought to be.
- An anxiety or fear of being crazy.
- A sense that time is passing and she's missing something.
- A desire not to be the way she is—"too sensitive," etc.
- A hesitancy to accept her perceptions.
- A reluctance to come to conclusions.
- A desire to escape or run away.
- A belief that what she does best may be what she does worst.
- A tendency to live in the future—"Everything will be great when/after . . ."
- A distrust of future relationships.

Sound familiar? It is conceivable that in perusing this chapter a reader might identify either a victim or a perpetrator of verbal abuse. Some readers may even question the possibility of abuse in their own lives. The following brief overviews of characteristics and categories of verbal abuse should help clarify this often overlooked form of violence. The lack of information addressing the subject of verbal abuse gives evidence to the fact that it is an often ignored plague. From those interested in understanding verbal abuse to the therapists working with its victims and abusers, all are indebted to Patricia Evans for her work on the subject. She details the following information:[7]

The General Characteristics of Verbal Abuse

- •Verbal abuse is hurtful.
- •Verbal abuse attacks the nature and abilities of the partner.
- •Verbal abuse may be overt (angry outbursts and name-calling) or covert (very subtle, like brainwashing).
- •Verbally abusive disparagement may be voiced in an extremely sincere and concerned way.
- •Verbal abuse is manipulative and controlling.
- •Verbal abuse is insidious.
- •Verbal abuse is unpredictable.
- •Verbal abuse is the issue (the problem) in the relationship.
- •Verbal abuse expresses a double message.
- •Verbal abuse usually escalates, increasing in intensity, frequency, and variety.

The Categories of Verbal Abuse

- •Withholding
- •Countering
- •Discounting
- •Verbal abuse disguised as jokes
- •Blocking and diverting
- •Accusing and blaming
- •Judging and criticizing
- •Trivializing
- •Undermining
- •Threatening
- •Name calling
- •Forgetting

•Ordering
•Denial
•Abusive anger

Clearly, verbal abuse is a complex issue. It is also one aspect of violence that needs attention from friends, family, the church, and the community. Abusers are typically in denial over this behavior. Their anger is unpredictable and irrational. Actions we take to assist victims of verbal abuse can eventually help reduce violence in our communities and thus help create a safer world.

When You or Someone You Know is Being Verbally Abused

•Get professional counseling support.
•Ask the mate of the abused person to go to this counselor also.
•Start setting limits.
•Stay in the present, trying to dwell neither on the past nor on concerns for the future.
•Be aware that people can leave any abusive situation.
•Ask for changes in the relationship.[8]

The unknown is frightening, and any change in a relationship is frightening. Even someone trapped in a verbally abusive relationship may find change frightening. Be an encourager to the victim. Refrain from judgment, criticism, and unsolicited advice, no matter how well meaning your intentions. Recognize that the healing process can take years. Survivors of verbal abuse give evidence that victims can attain wholeness and lives filled with joy and meaning.

Verbal Abuse and Children

A nationwide study involving over 3,300 children set out to determine the number of American children being verbally abused by their parents, the frequency of the attacks, and the correlation between the children's experiences and the high rate of childhood psychological and social problems. The summary and conclusion of the study revealed that:[9]

•Approximately two-thirds of American children are victims of verbal/symbolic aggression by parents.

•Verbal aggression by parents occurred an average of 12.6 times during the year of this study, and more than a third reported 11 or more instances.

•More boys are victims of verbal aggression than girls.

•More children over age six were likely to have experienced verbal aggression. However, if children under age six were the victims of verbal aggression, it occurred more frequently than was the case with children over age six.

Parental verbal aggression was directly related to the behavior problems of the child as follows:

•The more frequent the rate of verbal aggression by the parent, the greater the probability of physical, aggressive, or delinquent behavior by the child.

•Children who are never hit by their parents often exhibit behavior problems associated with verbal aggression.

•The correlation between verbal aggression and psychosocial problems affects all age groups, both sexes, and all families regardless of their socioeconomic status.

•The psychosocial problems of children are more directly related to parental verbal aggression than to physical aggression.

•Psychosocial behavior problems of children were found to be more directly affected by a combination of verbal aggression and abusive violence rather than experiencing either by itself.

While children are often targets of verbal abuse from their parents, the role of siblings is also important. According to psychologist Carol Wilson of the University of South Florida, Tampa, some parents may not realize the damaging power of verbal weapons their children use. In a September 9, 1997, article in *USA Today*, Wilson is quoted as saying: "Parents think these put-downs are childish and harmless because they wouldn't hurt an adult. But when they're hurled at kids by a sibling, they can really hurt."[10]

We cannot underestimate the role of the church and community in caring for children. We can begin to address the concern of children and verbal abuse through:

- Parenting classes.
- Mentoring programs for new and single parents.
- Support groups for parents and children.
- Professional counseling.
- Prayer!

The Abuser

While much of our attention has been and should be focused on victims of verbal abuse, no work on the subject would be complete without addressing the abuser. Most verbal abuse occurs in private. The abuser usually appears loving, caring, and supportive. He typically does not admit or recognize his abuse. Every abuser is different, just as every person is different. However, common characteristics indicate that the abuser may be:[11]

- irritable
- likely to blame his mate for his outbursts or actions
- unpredictable (you never know what will anger him)
- angry
- intense
- unaccepting of his mate's feelings and views
- inexpressive of warmth and empathy
- controlling
- silent and uncommunicative in private or frequently demanding or argumentative
- a "nice guy" to others
- competitive toward his partner
- sullen
- jealous
- quick with comebacks or put-downs

•critical
•manipulative
•explosive
•hostile
•inexpressive

Anyone can be the victim of verbal violence, and anyone can be a perpetrator. "Verbal abuse is symptomatic of personal, cultural, and global problems which originate with the misuse of power."[12] As more people become aware of the extent of this form of violence, its victims will become more comfortable in openly seeking help and wholeness. No one should have to live in the awful world of verbal abuse. If our goal involves creating a safer world, we must combat verbal abuse and its resulting emotional and psychological trauma.

BIBLICAL FOUNDATIONS

"Let my words . . . be pleasing to you, Lord" (Psalm 19:14 CEV).

Old Testament passages frequently employ the use of the phrase *word of God*. The purpose of each divine communication is to give a commandment, prophecy, warning, promise, or encouragement. God's example for us is that words should have a constructive purpose.[13]

Other Scriptures provide guidelines for our speech. Isaiah 30:10 is a reminder to speak pleasant words. Zechariah 8:16 calls us to speak the truth, be fair, and seek peace. Proverbs 10:19 and James 1:19 challenge us to be quick to hear, slow to speak, and slow to anger. Matthew 12:36 reminds us that we are accountable for careless words.

The biblical *word* cannot be separated from God's personal presence and power. In both Testaments, word is that through which God expresses Himself. God's creative word brought our universe into existence. His prophetic word unveils the future. His "ten words" outline His plan for moral order. He was ultimately revealed in Jesus, Who was eternal *logos* and flesh united in one. He was in the message about Jesus. God as a living person and as divine power finds expression in every word He utters.[14]

As a primer on proper verbal use, the Bible teaches us that every word is important. What we say is as important as how we say it. Our words should have a positive meaning and purpose. Ultimately our words are to praise God, testify to our experience with Christ, and build up one another. How different the world would be if this standard guided all speech. Words, once spoken, can never be taken back.

SEEKING SOLUTIONS

Church and community education play an essential role in seeking a solution to verbal abuse. When people recognize this form of violence for what it is and what it does, their awareness can result in intervention as well as prevention. Following is a list of specific actions individuals, families, groups, congregations, and communities can take to combat verbal abuse:

- •Conduct a "Sticks and Stones" awareness campaign. Utilize resources from this book to shed light on this dark and hidden form of violence.
- •Become an advocate for victims' rights.
- •Develop prevention programs for use in middle and high schools.
- •Educate clergy and lay leaders on ways to keep from adding to the victimization of verbal abuse.
- •Stop denying the reality of verbal abuse.
- •Host a support group.
- •Identify helping agencies in your community with training and resources to deal with the victim as well as the abuser.
- •Watch what you say!
- •Choose to create a safer world in your community.
- •Pray for an end to verbal abuse and all violence.

Ministry Models

Because people have only recently begun to recognize and talk about verbal abuse, few observable ministry models exist. Victims as well as abusers are, however, finding help through pastoral and clinical professional counselors who have adequate knowledge of verbal abuse and experience in assisting them on the road to recovery.

The support group experience can also be encouraging for victims and can provide a necessary community for validating feelings and facilitating growth and healing.

One-on-one mentoring or nurturing relationships can help build a healthy sense of self-worth in those who are abused. This nonthreatening situation allows individuals to set personal goals and have a built-in system of support and accountability.

Someone who has been verbally abused has lost her sense of self-worth and self-respect, and may believe she is unlovable. A women's Bible study group can offer nurture and support in helping her discover her worth in the sight of God.

"Yelling at living things does tend to kill the spirit in them. Sticks and stones may break our bones, but words will break our hearts."[15]

Chapter Twelve

PUT THE SPORT BACK IN SPORTS

By Don Walker

Hit 'em again, hit 'em again, harder . . . *harder!*" From the time our preschoolers enter the world of organized athletics, chants such as these emanate from the sidelines and bleachers. Overzealous parents take out their frustrations on officials, coaches, and children by screaming, cursing, and sometimes resorting to physical violence. On the way home after the game, these same angry parents voice disgust, make excuses, and assign blame. What began as family recreation becomes the battleground for alleviating parental frustration. All the while, innocent but observant children sit quietly by, wondering why playing isn't fun anymore. No wonder there is so much controversy surrounding athletics. Built on this kind of foundation, sports becomes a potential source of the problem of violence instead of a solution.

We are often critical of poor role models in college and professional ranks, but parents and coaches instill this behavior pattern well before children observe outsiders such as these. Parents teach throughout their children's years of participation in sports, and negative attitudes tend to escalate as children grow older. By the time our children reach high school, the stage is firmly set for a lifetime of emulating that most powerful of role models: the parent. Sadly, church-league athletic teams are often breeding grounds for poor sportsmanship from both players and parents. What ought to be an opportunity for light in a dark place becomes instead a playing field for behavior that is anything but Christlike. The actions and reactions of Christian parents and coaches are often no different—and sometimes much more violently pronounced—than their secular counterparts.

Organized sports provide people with opportunities to release energy, vent frustration, and curb violent tendencies. But have sports outlived their effectiveness in teaching young people valuable life skills such as discipline, teamwork, persistence, and physical well-being? Has one of the greatest mechanisms for teaching self-control become the problem instead of an answer? Jacksonville Jaguar tight end Rich Griffith used the term *controlled violence* to describe his involvement in football. "Yes, football is a violent sport," Griffith said. "But there are definite rules and officials who are charged with enforcing the rules. If I lose control and break the rules, the officials are there immediately to enforce the rules and levy penalties. They make sure the game is played in control." Certainly, we need opportunities to express ourselves and channel our energy in a "controlled" atmosphere. But how much more effectively could that happen in a Spirit-controlled atmosphere?

College athletes often become the focus at the mention of violence in sports. More often than not, the offenses concentrate on off-the-field activities such as fighting or rape. News accounts regularly report the arrest of professional athletes for committing violent acts, many of which are domestic. How would the stories of these role models have been different if as children, someone had helped build into their characters proper mechanisms for coping with stress, frustration, and loss of emotional control?

The greatest issue surrounding violence in sports is not violence as a result of sports but rather violence as a result of frustration, uncontrolled emotions, and an unwillingness to accept responsibility for one's actions.

BIBLICAL FOUNDATIONS

Sports and athletics were clearly an important part of the culture and society in which the Bible was penned. Significant Bible teachings center around athletics or use athletic themes. While there are no direct biblical references to violence as it relates to sports, the Bible abounds with teachings relevant to the athlete. Every serious athlete is driven by the pursuit of excellence, which the Bible encourages and directs. Philipians 4:8 states: "Finally, brothers, whatever is true, whatever is noble, whatever is right, whatever is pure, whatever is lovely, whatever is admirable—if anything is excellent or praiseworthy—think about such things." This verse becomes the gauge by which athletes can measure themselves against God's standard. The words of 1 Corinthians 10:31*b* are painted on the walls of more than one locker room to spur on excellence: "Whatever you do, do it all for the glory of God."

Being the best is the dream of every athlete, yet few ever achieve such a level of performance. Performance itself causes stress in athletes' lives. Anytime we get more interested in what we do (performance) than who we are (personhood), we are in a position for upset. Paul reminds us in 2 Corinthians 5:17: "Therefore, if anyone is in Christ, he is a new creation; the old has gone, the new has come!" Who we are or become in Christ completes the pursuit of the abundant life. What we do becomes secondary to who we are in Him. Our motivation changes. We are motivated by devotion to Jesus Christ, the greatest motivator who ever lived. He faced every obstacle people can face, yet He did not fail. He serves as the highest model for excellence, persistence, patience, and freedom from the obstacles that keep us from becoming the best we can be.

Other strong biblical teachings relate to sacrifice, commitment, discipline, persistence, and character. All of these are keys to building a healthy attitude and a strategy for dealing with the threat of uncontrolled violence in sports. The Bible likewise speaks volumes about controlling our emotions, dealing with frustration, and living with the consequences of our actions. Mark 12:31*a* teaches us to "Love your neighbor as yourself." Many people turn to athletic achievement to build their own sense of self-worth. Clearly, we cannot love others if we do not love ourselves. This one concept is critical to curbing the wave of sports-related violence. When people learn to love themselves because of the love God has shown them, every relationship in which they are involved is affected. Spouses love each other more completely. Parents and children love more fully. Friends and acquaintances love more genuinely. All relationships are more honest, fulfilling, and complete in Christ.

The Spirit-filled Christian, under the control of the Holy Spirit of God, lives by the theme of "not I, but Christ in me." That principle can revolutionize our lives by helping us control our emotions. When God's Spirit is in control, One Who knows our capabilities to handle stressful situations leads us. He directs us down straight paths of righteousness.

The Bible is purposed and full of concrete instructions concerning consequences for actions. None is more pronounced than Romans 6:23*a*: "For the wages of sin is death." The consequences of our mistakes, poor choices, and out-of-control behavior are clear. There is a price to pay for "playing" outside of the rules God has established. The penalty flags have been thrown. God has an answer!

Concerned Christians are involved in a variety of ministries to help athletes and coaches deal with specific issues that are present in athletics. Groups such as the Fellowship of Christian Athletes and others work to bring Christ into the world of athletics. These groups specialize in reaching into this specific venue of influence and challenging people to take seriously the claims of Christ. They exist to spread the gospel, influence the sports world, and funnel young men and women into the fellowship of a local church.

SEEKING SOLUTIONS

Athletics and faith clearly have strong parallels. It is no wonder that the Bible is filled with so many teachings that are communicated with athletic themes. For years, international missionaries have used sports programs and athletics as means to the end of presenting the gospel and leading people in Christian discipleship. Some have discovered that athletics can even open the doors to many countries that are closed to a traditional Christian missionary presence. Events such as the Olympic games and other international competitions also provide Christians with opportunities for ministry and witness to those who might otherwise never hear the gospel message. Likewise, today's churches can use the avenues of sports and athletics as tools for reaching their communities with the gospel.

Some churches have been involved in sports and recreation ministries for years. Unfortunately, many see these only as providing opportunities for people to participate. They do not realize the responsibility and power of using the arena of athletics to present the gospel message in a culturally relevant and powerful way.

Many coaches fail to fully understand the power of their influence. According to one poll, when asked about the most influential adult in their lives, 80 percent of teenagers named a coach. Consider this possibility: The average Little League baseball team has between 10 and 20 players. Each player comes from a family of anywhere from 2 to 10 people. On one little league team alone, a coach can potentially influence between 20 and 200 individuals. Assuming that each league has 10 teams, a church could have the potential to influence up to 2,000 individuals with the message of Christ!

Amazing opportunities exist for churches that select and train coaches not only in the skills of coaching but in the art of pastoral ministry. Families feel the need to provide excellent activities for their children. Churches have the answer: quality Christian sports leagues coached by carefully selected and trained Christian men and women. Some of the best experiences my children have had on sports teams have come from coaches whose intentions are not only to coach the sport but also to teach values and character and to live out their Christian commitment on the field of play. Teams coached by men and women with these intentions produce players who are in control of their emotions and display good sportsmanship. And they encourage parents and other spectators to do the same.

Churches have the opportunity to provide training that can not only help combat the problem of violence in sports but can bring resolution to the issue by dealing with violence from an eternal perspective. Many sports organizations require a certain number of hours of skills training in order for a coach to be certified. Churches can develop coaching clinics not only for their own programs but for community coaches as well. In addition to skills training, they can offer seminars related to developing and nurturing players' self-esteem, helping children deal with disappointment and frustration, exhibiting good sportsmanship in both winning and losing, and dealing effectively with parents and colleagues.

The secular world makes many attempts to confront the escalation of violence. Currently, schools in our area are participating in programs such as Victory Over Violence that emphasize four principles of action:

- Praise People (have a positive attitude);
- Give Up Put-downs (don't put others down to make yourself look better);
- Notice Hurts and Right Wrongs (apologize and make it right);
- Seek Wise People (look to parents, teachers, coaches, or others for help).

These four principles have parallel applications for Christian coaches. Churches can easily adapt and use these principles as the basis for developing a church-based coaching clinic:

Self-confidence and self-worth are positive outcomes of athletics, and the concept of praise is a key factor in their development. All children need to receive praise. But coaches and players alike need to develop a deeper understanding of praise. God deserves praise in all circumstances, including the highs and lows of athletic competition. God makes some extraordinary promises to those who obey His principles. When we align our priorities with God's principles, He blesses us. Matthew 6:33 reminds us to "seek first his kingdom and his righteousness, and all these things will be given to you as well." When we praise God in all things, including the ups and downs of coaching and playing sports, God promises that we will know abundant living.

The concept of "giving up put-downs" is rooted in Scripture. Paul reminds us in 1 Thessalonians 5:11 to "encourage one another and build each other up." Any activity the church undertakes should purposely build up, rather than tear down, others. Any activity of an individual Christian believer should aim toward that intended result as well. Christian coaches have a wonderful opportunity to help build up young players and to model for them how to encourage and build up others, regardless of the score.

The sporting principle of "notice hurts and right wrongs" also has great implications for Christian coaches. Team sports provide opportunities for coaches and players to focus less on their individual needs and hurts and more on those of the whole team. Following Christ produces the spiritual sensitivity to see others through the eyes of Christ, discover hurts and wrongs, and work to correct them, just as Christ would do.

The fourth principle needs little interpretation. "Seek wise people" is strong biblical advice. We need each other. We need the accountability that comes as "iron sharpens iron." We need to encourage coaches to hold each other accountable for the messages they present to children. Parents need to hold each other accountable for their words and actions before, during, and after games. And on a deeper level, we need to understand the true source of wisdom. James 1:5 tells us, "If any of you lacks wisdom, he should ask God, who gives generously to all without finding fault, and it will be given to him." God is not only the source of wisdom, He is wisdom.

The church has an awesome door of opportunity to use the influence of sports to effect changes in our culture. Matthew 28:18–20 is our missions mandate and standard. A. C. Queen, a retired missionary to Cuba, explained these verses to me when I was a young campus minister in a way that changed my life. People often interpret the words "Go therefore" as a mandate to go somewhere else and share the gospel, he said. In fact, the translation might more accurately be stated something like this: "Since you are already going about the daily affairs of life anyway, make disciples!"

In the ordinary comings and goings of our lives, we develop enough relationships with people who do not know Christ personally to keep us busy witnessing for a long time. Those who are involved in sports either as a participant, as a parent, or as a coach can adopt their team and the many relationships it provides as their missions field. Instead of asking God to bring people into our lives to whom we can witness, we more rightly pray when we ask God to open our eyes to opportunities we already have on a daily basis. What a concept—sports evangelism!

Chapter Thirteen

CONTROL THE TELEVISION CONTROLS

By James Spann

I will never forget the sick feeling in my stomach when I heard the news. The television station where I had worked for seven years was being sold. There was a good chance that, when the sale was complete, the network affiliation would change to one whose programming standards I could not endorse. As the chief meteorologist for this station, I had worked long hours to convince people of all ages, from children to senior adults, to watch our station. I spent a part of every weekday (on my own time, by the way) on the road, speaking to schools, churches, and civic groups, helping to build the station into a ratings powerhouse.

First I tried to convince myself that the shows on this other network weren't so bad. After all, I really hadn't watched that many of its programs, and maybe their reputation of "pushing the envelope" with shows glamorizing sex and violence wasn't warranted. After a week of watching the network, however, I knew I didn't want to be associated with it. It seemed to me that it was building its programming around values that destroy rather than nurture families, and that promote violence rather than peace.

About nine months later, we learned that this network was actually buying our station. So instead of just being an affiliate, we would be owned and operated by the network. This

105

was a real dilemma, since I loved working for the station and had many good friends there. After long hours of prayer, I felt like the right thing to do was resign. Going out on the street and encouraging people to watch that type of programming, in my opinion, would damage my Christian witness. I knew the Lord had better plans for me. So the day of the switch, I resigned, despite legal tangles with a contract dispute. I was hired one month later by a new major network affiliate in the same city. To my amazement, about four weeks after accepting that position, this network announced that the main character in one of its prime time series would "come out of the closet" as a homosexual at the end of the television season. The station I had recently joined was the only affiliate in the nation to have the courage not to air this episode. Our management asked the network for permission to air the show after the family viewing period, but the network refused. Thus, this episode was not seen in our market at that time, despite heavy protest from the local gay and lesbian community and the local print media.

With each passing year, it seems that television networks set a new standard for immoral programming. It is time for Christians to draw a line in the sand and separate ourselves from sex and violence on television. Consider these key findings from the Mediascope National Television Violence Study, released in February 1996:[1]

1. The context in which most television violence is presented poses risks for viewers. The majority of programs analyzed in the study contain violence, but more important is the context for these acts of violence. By watching common depictions of violence, viewers risk:
•Learning to behave violently.
•Becoming more desensitized to violence.
•Becoming more fearful of being attacked.

The contextual patterns recur across most channels, program types, and times of day. That means there are substantial risks of harmful effects from viewing violence throughout the television environment.

2. **Perpetrators go unpunished in 73 percent of all violent scenes.** When violence is presented without punishment, viewers are more likely to learn the lesson that violence is successful.

3. **In all, 47 percent of all violent interactions show no harm to victims and 58 percent show no pain.** Only 16 percent of all programs portray the long-term negative effects of violence, such as psychological, financial, or emotional harm.

4. **A total of 25 percent of violent interactions on television involve handguns.**

5. **Only 4 percent of violent programs emphasize an anti-violence theme.**

6. **Television violence is not usually explicit or graphic.** Less than 3 percent of violent scenes feature close-ups of violence, and only 15 percent contain blood and gore.

7. **The industry norm for television violence is 57 percent of programming, but there are notable differences in how violence is presented across television channels.** Public broadcasting has the least risk of harmful effect with 18 percent of its programming being violent. On premium cable channels, 85 percent of programming is violent with the highest risk of harmful effect. On broadcast networks 44 percent of programming is violent, and the context for these depictions is as problematic as on other channels.

8. **There are important differences in the presentation of violence across types of television programs.** Movies are most likely to present violence in realistic settings (85 percent of the time), and to include blood and gore in violent scenes (28 percent of the time). Children's programs are the least likely of all genres to show the long-term negative consequences of violence (5 percent of the time), and they frequently portray violence in a humorous context (67 percent of the time).

Television is certainly not the only media outlet that offers violence on a regular basis. Many American homes now have access to the Internet. While this can be a great resource for families and children, it also offers a bizarre array of Web sites involving everything from pornography to how to make a pipe bomb. And have you listened to the lyrics on some alternative radio stations lately? Songs that make rape and acts of violence seem right are everywhere on these stations. Beyond that, it is hard to find a movie these days that doesn't show at least one or two murders.

BIBLICAL FOUNDATIONS

Is media violence really harmful? Yes. What we see in movies and on television often shapes our thought processes which, in turn, can affect our behavior. Spiritual warfare begins with control of the mind. Philippians 4:8 says: "Finally, brothers, whatever is true, whatever is noble, whatever is right, whatever is pure, whatever is lovely, whatever is admirable—if anything is excellent or praiseworthy—think about such things." Music, movies, and television programs that glamorize violence don't fall in the category of pure, lovely, admirable, excellent, or praiseworthy.

Listen to the words of Jesus from Mark 9:43–47:

> "If your hand causes you to sin, cut it off. It is better for you to enter life maimed than with two hands to go into hell, where the fire never goes out. And if your foot causes you to sin, cut it off. It is better for you to enter life crippled than to have two feet and be thrown into hell. And if your eye causes you to sin, pluck it out. It is better for you to enter the kingdom of God with one eye than to have two eyes and be thrown into hell."

Is Jesus instructing us to literally cut off body parts? No. Jesus is telling us to cut out the things in our lives that bring temptation and sin. These can include a television program, a movie, a Web site, or even certain types of music. Many murderers on death row have confessed that the idea of murder started by a simple thought brought on from an act of violence they witnessed on television or in a movie.

SEEKING SOLUTIONS

The problem of violence in the media has been around for a long time, and the search for an answer to the problem continues. One of the more recent solutions from the television industry is its voluntary ratings system, which rates each show based on the opinion of the producers, networks, and others that originate programs. Critics of this plan want the shows to be independently rated, and there is some merit to their argument. Knowing the anti-Christian values of some of the people who produce and write television shows today, I'm not so sure I want them rating the programs themselves. But on the other hand, at least this is a start. Here is the rating scheme in place at this writing:

TV-Y: Material suitable for children of all ages. Themes and elements in programs with this rating are specifically designed for a very young audience, including children from ages 2 to 6.

TV-Y7: Material suitable for children age seven and above. Themes and elements in this program may include mild physical or comedic violence, or may frighten children under the age of 7.

TV-G: Material suitable for all audiences. Contains little or no violence, no strong language, and little or no sexual dialogue or situations.

TV-PG: Parental guidance is suggested. Program may contain infrequent coarse language, limited violence, and some suggestive sexual dialogue and situations.

TV-14: Material may be inappropriate for children under 14.

Program may contain sophisticated themes, strong language, sexual content, and more intense violence.

TV-M: For mature audiences only. Program may contain mature themes, profane language, graphic violence, and explicit sexual content.

As a parent, I want to give this system a try. Look for the small rating logo on the screen at the beginning of each program. Let it help you make the decision about watching the program. But again, don't let that rating be your only guide. The system isn't perfect and has a long way to go, but it is, at least, a start. The next big development in parental control will be the V chip, which is an electronic board that will be included in future television receivers. This will allow viewers to block display of all programs with a common rating. The V chip concept is part of the Telecommunications Act of 1996 (section 551), where the Congress of the United States made the following findings:[2]

Television influences children's perception of the values and behavior that are common and acceptable in society.

Television station operators, cable television system operators, and video programmers should take into consideration the fact television programming has established a uniquely pervasive presence in the lives of American children.

The average American child is exposed to 25 hours of television each week. Some children are exposed to as much as 11 hours of television a day.

Studies have shown that children exposed to violent video programming at a young age have a higher tendency for violent and aggressive behavior later in life than children not so exposed, and that children exposed to violent video programming are prone to assume that acts of violence are acceptable behavior.

Children in the United States are, on average, exposed to an estimated 8,000 murders and 100,000 acts of violence on television by the time they complete elementary school.

Studies indicate that children are affected by the pervasiveness and casual treatment of sexual material on television, eroding the ability of parents to develop responsible attitudes and behavior in their children.

Parents express grave concern over violent and sexual video programming and strongly support technology that would give them greater control over what may be harmful to their children.

There is a compelling governmental interest in empowering parents to limit the negative influences of video programming that is harmful to children.

Providing parents with timely information about the nature of upcoming video programming and with the technological tools that allow them easily to block violent, sexual, or other programming that they believe harmful to their children is a nonintrusive and narrowly tailored means of achieving that compelling governmental interest.

While the V chip could be a huge help in preventing television violence from coming into our homes, we still must be actively involved as parents and adults. One group engaged in this pursuit is TV-Free America, a national nonprofit, non-partisan organization that encourages Americans to voluntarily and dramatically reduce the amount of television that they watch in order to promote richer, healthier, and more connected lives, and to promote families and communities.[3]

This organization sponsors National TV-Turnoff Week, a nationwide effort that focuses attention not on the quality of television programming but on the excessive quantity of television that most Americans watch. It asks that people reassess the role television plays in their daily lives as entertainer, baby-sitter, time filler, sales force, and background noise. National TV-Turnoff Week is about becoming re-engaged in your community.

For two years, the National TV-Turnoff Week has been an overwhelming success. More than 8 million people (and 45,000 schools) around the country and abroad have taken part in this event and experienced simpler, healthier, and more relaxed and productive lives. Thousands have reported a wide range of benefits, including increased family interaction and community involvement.

As an employee of a television station (I mean, this industry feeds my family!), the concept is a bit scary to me. On the other hand, it is a fascinating concept: spending time talking with your spouse and children with no interruption from the television. This National TV-Turnoff Week concept could change your life, and is sure worth a try. We might even take this a step further: try eliminating television, radio, movies, and the Internet for an entire week. You might learn things about your family you never knew before!

While the turn-off concept sounds great, we are all aware that the media is a big part of our lives, and it won't go away. As Christians concerned about the future of what we see and hear from the media giants, we must be more active in letting the program producers know what we like and what we don't like.

Here are some guidelines on how you can help quality, family-oriented programs and movies become greater in number:

Don't watch programs that glorify violence. The most powerful statement you can make is with the channel switch. If a television program has low ratings, it will soon be gone. If a movie is a box office flop, it won't be on the screen for long. *You* are the key player here. If a movie or program is telling you that violent acts are normal behavior, don't even think about watching it again. And pass the word to all your friends and family members. You might think you are the last Christian in this country based on what the media is telling you, but don't believe it. There is power in numbers, and there is still a large number of God-fearing people in our nation.

Note the advertisers that support offensive programs and don't support them. In addition, write them a note and let them know you don't approve of their endorsement of violence by spending their advertising budget on programs like that.

Purposefully watch family-oriented programs and programs that portray Christianity positively. It is easy to throw out a blanket indictment of the television industry, but the truth is that there are still some excellent family-oriented series on the air, even on the major networks. If we don't watch these shows, they will simply go away as the moral climate continues to deteriorate. Do your homework, and search out these programs. Television programs live and die by ratings! If by chance you have a meter from the A. C. Neilson Company, you are one of the most powerful television households in America! Your viewing will have a direct impact on the final numbers and the ultimate destination of the program. The same holds true for movies; when you see a G-rated movie, take the children and enjoy it! If Hollywood makes money on a family movie, they will consider doing one like it again. Stay away from the trash talk shows. It is difficult to understand how any human can watch the "freak of the week" shows every weekday on local stations. Even some of these shows considered to be "classy" have become beacons for the promotion of homosexuality, New Age religion, and other anti-Christian values. This stuff is scary, and the only way to make these shows go away (or change their tune) is to turn them off.

Do your homework before choosing a station for your local TV news source. Know the owners and management of each local station in your market. There are some stations that are much more family-friendly than others. Does your preferred station for local news have a full-time reporter that covers Christian issues? My station employs a reporter who does a series called "Matters of Faith." This is one of the most popular franchise reports we have on the air. We need to support local stations that appreciate and boost family values.

As we become active in making an effort to reduce violence in the media, we must remember it is not our place to condemn or judge other people. We clearly must take a stand against violence, but it won't work if we attack individuals. This includes television station managers, producers, talk show hosts, and reporters. Several years ago, I drove to work through a group of Christians who were near the entrance to the station to protest the airing of a particular show. I remember seeing them shout at me, pointing fingers and looking like crazy people. That is not the way to change someone's heart. Their actions only damaged my ability to share my faith with the non-Christians who had to drive through their demonstrations. It is our job to develop a relationship with lost people and then share the gospel as God allows. We must never forget that we *all* are sinners. We are not on some different human level, although we, of course, are saved by God's grace. Once we put ourselves on some "holier than thou" pedestal, we can forget being good witnesses.

As Christians, we can make a difference in our children and our families by educating ourselves about media violence and by taking responsible steps to curtail that violence. And when we limit our children's exposure to violence in all its forms, we not only protect them, we make a better world.

Chapter Fourteen

DIFFUSE WORKPLACE DISAGREEMENTS

By Lowell Lawson

"Postal Clerk Kills 15!"

"Twenty-eight Die in Fast Food Shooting."

"Auto Worker Guns Down Supervisor, Office Staff."

Headlines such as these are no longer uncommon. Consequently, they seldom shock us. But workplace violence, though it is not at epidemic proportions, occurs often enough to concern everyone.

A popular major league manager summarizes his leadership style this way: "My way or the highway." More and more frequently, individuals respond to this authoritarian style with a confrontational philosophy: "My way or the die-way."

Historically, people of differing opinions have sought to discuss, negotiate, and resolve differences in verbal or other nonviolent ways. Today, resolution too often comes in the form of violent behavior that may be lethal.

The workplace is a prime arena for violence. Employed adults spend the major portion of their waking time at work. Pressure to produce, an impersonal setting, and insensitive supervision can nurture feelings of inadequacy in employees. Limited opportunities for advancement, lack of recognition for a job well done, and the need for additional income to meet expenses create strong internal pressures.

A person's job, his or her means of supporting self and family, is one of life's most personal aspects. For many people, their job is their identity. What they do is who they are.

115

When a person's job is threatened, negatively modified, or lost, that person can easily become desperate. Violence can follow. The inability, real or perceived, to find a listening ear lights the spark that ignites the inferno raging within an individual. The natural targets of attack are those perceived to have caused the emotional distress.

Even individuals whose work offers only brief contact with others can face workplace violence. Drunken passengers assault airline flight attendants. Hostile riders shoot cab drivers. Angry parents and fans attack umpires and referees because of an unpopular decision. Irate drivers en route to work shoot other motorists who vie for a space on an exit ramp from the highway.

Violence in the workplace comes in all kinds of packages. Fortunately, most instances do not result in tragedies that make news headlines. A disgruntled employee slams the door on his way out of an office. Two workers on an assembly line share their dislike for a supervisor. One punctuates his remarks by saying, "I'd like to meet him in a dark alley." Significant acts of violence in the workplace are, however, on the rise. Fired employees return to their office and kill co-workers, secretaries, managers, and anyone whom they believe had a part in the loss of their livelihood. The possibilities for workplace violence are infinite. No one works in a totally safe place.

BIBLICAL FOUNDATIONS

Biblical events did not happen in an industrial setting. The world was a simple place then. Work, for the most part, was in the fields, although there were some small businesses. Men fished for food and for a living. It was a different culture and a different day. But the elements for workplace discord were then, in many ways, the same as today. Dissatisfaction with wages, jealousy, oppressive bosses, and unfair labor practices created disharmony in the biblical workshop.

The Bible even records an instance of workplace violence. The first two persons born on earth provide us with a classic case. Cain and his brother, Abel, labored in the fields. The farmer realized the shepherd's gift to God was superior to his. His jealousy led him to commit the first murder. No newspaper headlines. No six o'clock news story. Cain thought no one saw it. God did.

Today a worker is bypassed for a promotion. Jealousy develops. The response is to kill the one promoted and the one promoting. Thousands of years apart. Different time, same crime.

The Bible addresses the relationship between workers and employers in many places, and its teaching is constant. Workers and employers should have a fair relationship. The Bible tells us the worker is worthy of his wages (1 Tim. 5:18) and that fair pay is due for a fair day's work (James 5:1–4). It further teaches us to work hard, to respect others who also do so, and to live in peace (1 Thess. 5:12–13). The Bible does not teach violence. It teaches that we are to get along with each other.

SEEKING SOLUTIONS

Violence in the workplace is a high-priority concern at many levels. Business and industry, supervisory personnel, and assembly line workers give it high priority. Sensitive professionals such as psychologists, psychiatrists, school counselors, ministers, and pastoral counselors are finding ways to address the problem. Those who are not in job classifications that might mark them as potential targets for violence still care and seek solutions.

Responses to violence may be reactive (those that take place after the fact) or proactive (those that are taken before a violent act occurs). Proactive steps do not guarantee that violence will not occur, but they do help minimize its impact.

Of course, it is desirable that reactive programs be unnecessary. However, there are few events so devastating to individuals as workplace violence. An act of workplace violence can totally shut down an individual's life or place of business. Sometimes its effects can last a lifetime.

Despite the ever-present possibility of workplace violence, it inevitably takes everyone by tragic surprise. Chaos initially occurs. Depending on the scope, nature, and setting of the violence, the time to restore order, resolve the conflict, and return to normalcy may vary greatly. The suicide of a discharged employee in his parked car, miles from the workplace, will have a lesser impact than the killing of a foreman in the plant during the middle of the workday.

Critical Incident Stress Debriefing (CISD) teams are effective ways to address workplace violence. Organized and trained to deal with sudden violent situations, team members are equipped to meet with those who have been touched by an act of violence.

CISD team members are representative of the workplace and the professional community and often include chaplains and pastors. Through extensive group meetings, such teams lead individuals to share their grief and other emotions and move toward a healing that will enable them to function effectively in the workplace again.

Churches can sponsor special group sessions for church and nonchurch members who have been touched by workplace violence. Violence knows no denomination. Pastors, members with appropriate training in grief counseling, and community professionals can give leadership to these groups.

There are even more opportunities to address workplace violence proactively. One rapidly growing approach is to place chaplains in business and industrial settings. Because they are intimately familiar with the setting, they are especially effective in defusing critical situations as they talk with persons who feel aggrieved and with coworkers and supervisory personnel. They are sensitive to potentially violent personalities and workplace situations. These chaplains may be laypersons, bivocational ministers in the workplace, or clergy and pastoral counselors who serve on a part-time or full-time salaried basis.

Preparing for workplace violence is no guarantee that it will not happen. But it may prevent some incidents or, at least, provide a quick and meaningful response if they do occur. Churches can address workplace violence by:

Participating in CISD teams. Church members can become members of a CISD team by contacting leadership of existing CISD teams in the community. Learn about the functions of the CISD team and take the training that is required. You can find these teams by contacting your local regional emergency medical service system.

Conducting awareness classes. Churches can offer seminars, conferences, discussion groups, and special classes addressing workplace violence. Often, church members can provide leadership for these events. Many agencies and businesses can also provide expertise. While those who have never experienced it may show indifference toward discussing workplace violence, others will have some awareness of its potential. Some people will welcome the opportunity to discuss it, address their concerns, and be better prepared to defuse potentially violent circumstances. Employees, clients, customers, students, the walk-in public, and emotionally disturbed individuals may give expression to feelings of anger and frustration at anytime in the least expected places. Violence can also erupt in school classrooms, playgrounds, worship services, and quiet restaurants. The common reaction is, "How could it happen here?" The truth is, workplace violence can happen anywhere.

Forming support groups. When an act of workplace violence occurs, the individuals directly involved are not the only ones who are affected. Everyone even remotely touched by the incident will experience reactions. An effective means of dealing with physical and emotional needs is through small groups. Depending on the nature of the incident and the depth of its impact, the group(s) may meet for one time or for an extended series of meetings. The opportunity to verbalize feelings and reactions and share personal experiences is one of the most important facets of the healing process.

Offering post-incident ministries. Churches can be supportive of businesses and employees that have experienced
workplace violence in a number of ways:

Letters. Individuals, Sunday School classes, missions groups,
and congregational letters will have great meaning to
those whose lives have been disrupted by violence.
Memorial services. Special worship services to honor those
who have died in an incident can go far to help survivors
and close associates of victims.
Benevolent expressions. Many of the ways churches express
support for those who have lost loved ones are welcomed
ministries to those who have experienced workplace violence. Providing meals and sending flowers, letters, and
cards of love and condolence will mean much to those
survivors and family members.
At an appropriate time the church can host a dinner or buffet
meal for those affected by a violent act. This corporate
expression of caring by a church, even and especially
when those to whom it ministers are not church members, can communicate Christ's love more than a thousand sermons or weekly telecasts of Sunday worship
services.

Workplace violence, as devastating and horrible as it is,
provides Christians with unusual opportunities to minister
and witness. This chapter suggests ways individuals, groups,
and entire congregations can do just that. But well-inten-
tioned people sometimes add to the problems of those who
have experienced workplace violence by using religious
clichés, overidentifying with victims and survivors, and expressing unrealistic hopes and expectations.

As you work both reactively and proactively to combat
workplace violence, consider the following do's and don'ts:

DON'T . . .
Use poor theology. Many people are ready to see the
immediate judgment of God in any negative experience
in life. God certainly has the power to make any event

occur, but He does not arbitrarily decide that anyone should suffer. Within His permissive will, bad things happen to good people. People wreak havoc in the lives of others. Because it happens does not mean God approves it.

Minimize the loss and hurt victims have experienced. "Time heals." "Well, you still have three other children." "I remember when my grandmother died last summer." Comments like these, while they are intended to comfort the hurting, often have the opposite effect. It is impossible to understand the distress of those touched by an act of violence. No one else's experiences can compare with those who are suffering. Even though your experience may have been more serious, at this particular moment the spotlight is brilliant and narrow. It exposes only one experience. That experience is not yours. Focus on the one who is hurting.

Be judgmental. "If you hadn't taken that job . . ." "If you had told your supervisor about that guy's weird behavior . . ." "If the company had only listened to you . . ." Twenty/twenty hindsight is wonderful. Unfortunately, we always have it too late! Victims of workplace violence are perfectly capable of expressing 20/20 hindsight. They do not need anyone else's input.

DO . . .

Become a caring presence. Some Christians think, "I don't like to visit hospitals or go to funerals. I don't know what to say." The number of Christians who avoid ministry to the sick, hospitalized, and bereaved is greater than we want to believe. "I don't know what to say" is a common excuse. At a time of crisis, your presence is more important than your words.

Remember that in reality, there are no special words, no phrases, nothing that can be spoken that can dispel human grief. Christ could say, "Young man, I say to you, get up" (Luke 7:14) and "My child, get up!" (Luke 8:54), and the dead walked. Our words are comforting, but they are not miraculous. In times of death and serious injury, a massive expression of sympathy usually follows. The bereaved are often unaware of all who came to see them. They remember little of what people say to them. What they remember is the love and support that surrounded them—a handshake, a hug, or a shared tear expressing love and care.

Remember that the hurting lasts a long time. An act of violence generally lasts a few seconds. Recovery from it can last a lifetime. The immediate response is important. However, the most significant ministry may well be that which will follow weeks, months, and even years after. Continuing to listen to, pray for, and remember on special occasions the victims and survivors of workplace violence demonstrates that we understand the depths of the hurts.

Workplace violence occurs unexpectedly. If we wait until it happens to prepare for ministry, our response will likely be slower and less effective than it could be. Ministry in these situations should be like the fire extinguisher in place on the wall. Hopefully, we will never need it. But when we do, it should be in working order. If we are ready, individual Christians and congregations will, through their caring responses, preach the greatest sermon many will ever hear.

Chapter Fifteen

DEVELOP A HEART TO HELP THE POOR

By Ken Weathersby

With whom do you associate the term *poverty*?" Although the responses to my informal survey question varied, the first response was usually something like this: "I see dirty children with dirty clothes." Others indicated that they see:

•the homeless, standing on street corners, begging for money or holding signs that read *Will Work for Food.*
•poor children afraid to walk home from school due to fear of violence.
•women afraid to get married because the government may disallow assistance or reduce the amount.
•children eating all they can at school because they may not receive another meal at home.
•teenagers selling drugs to try to make money.
•youth dropping out of school to work.
•young girls and women selling their bodies.
•homeless people sleeping under bridges or in parks.

Such are the faces of poverty in America's major urban centers, but do these same conditions cross the borders into rural America? Recent statistics reveal that the rural poor are more likely to:[1]

•dwell in inadequate housing.
•experience poverty on an annual cycle, as in the case of seasonal farm workers.

•be physically disabled.
•be too young or too old to hold regular employment.
•lack transportation resources to employment sites.
•be the "working poor," toiling at low-paying, seasonal jobs that do not provide enough income to secure adequate housing.
•lack access to health care services.
•be undereducated.

While it is difficult to imagine, there are people in America, the land of freedom and justice for all, who have no shelter, no food, and inadequate clothing. Over 32 million people live in poverty in our nation.[2] The Christian community has a biblical mandate to respond. Our response begins with becoming more sensitized to the needs of the poor and helping meet their immediate physical needs. It continues as we seek to meet their spiritual needs and provide them with opportunities to develop a personal relationship with Jesus Christ. And it comes full circle when we provide them a network to job employment preparation and placement and equip them with the tools that they need to avoid exploitation.

Poverty is the lack of means to provide material needs and comforts. It is a relative condition correlated with a standard of income. The official poverty line is based on a predetermined measure of financial resources needed for adequate nutrition and other basic needs.

Poverty has been classified as a set of behavioral characteristics associated with an inferior quality of life. Studies related to the culture of poverty imply that there are differences in attitudes, motivation, and social concerns related to crime, illegitimate births, mental illness, and family instability.[3]

Many victims of the cycle of poverty have not experienced freedom through a personal relationship with Christ. The Apostle Paul stated that whatever his circumstances he would be content (Phil. 4:11). No one can know contentment until he or she learns to focus on the things of God. "The fear of the Lord is the beginning of wisdom, and the knowledge of the Holy One is understanding" (Prov. 9:10). From a socio-logical perspective, poverty represents the separation of rela-tionships, knowledge, and understanding. It is, therefore, imperative that the focus on poverty shift from an internal one of helplessness to an eternal one of hopefulness.

As the condition of poverty has intensified over the years, so has the government's attempts at response. President Johnson declared war on poverty in 1964. Since then, the United States government has spent an estimated $1 trillion to lift the poor out of poverty, creating more than 100 government social agencies toward the effort.[4]

But we are losing the war on poverty, according to Tony Evans, author of *America's Only Hope*.

> "One out of every four American children lives in poverty. The elderly account for 35 percent of the poor. Those benefiting least are women, who now make up 77 percent of this country's poor."[5]

In 1994, $5 trillion were spent and 14.6 million children still lived in poverty. That figure constitutes a little more than one in every five American children.[6]

"The welfare system designed to help the poor has in reality helped to destroy them. It has killed their initiative," according to Evans. "Welfare itself has become like a drug that gives a quick fix but in the long run destroys."[7]

BIBLICAL FOUNDATIONS

God really cares about the poor; therefore, He wants His people to do the same, asserts Roland Sider in *Rich Christians in an Age of Hunger*. God expects believers to have a special affinity for the poor and weak. God even selected poor slaves in Egypt to be His chosen people.[8]

During the period of the Judges, God ordained that the poor be given full protection (Ex. 23:3; Deut. 16:19; Psalm 82:3). He ordered that interest not be exacted from the poor (Ex. 22:25; Deut. 23:20). The impoverished had the opportunity to glean in the field and vineyard (Deut. 24:19; cf. Ruth). However, there were no free rides. They were expected to work for their food. They were to be faithful to the commands and covenants of God.

Not everyone is poor for the same reason, and the Bible recognizes this fact. Some people are poor because they are lazy (Prov. 6:10–11; 15:19; 19:15; 24:30–31). Laziness casts one into a deep sleep, prohibiting the development of a productive experience, the Bible says. God detests laziness! He expects us to have the desire to work. Others who are poor have become skillful at manipulating the system to get what they want without having to work. In 2 Thessalonians 3:10b, Paul said, "If a man will not work, he shall not eat." God does not expect His church to enable laziness and irresponsibility. We use our ministry resources most wisely when we authenticate needs and unleash the financially paralyzed rather than perpetuate their dependence upon welfare.

Some are entangled in the web of drunkenness and stubbornness (Prov. 13:18; 28:19). Some misuse the resources God has provided to support their alcoholism. Many use alcohol as a camouflage for personal tragedy and failure that only masks the pain for a moment.

Still others experience poverty because of oppression and greed (Ex. 1:12–13; 2 Sam. 12:1–2; Jer. 22:13). The Bible routinely accounts God's deliverance of His people from oppression. Unfortunately, today some who are rich exploit the poor simply because they can; they are in positions of authority. The church has and must accept its responsibility to help the poor who are oppressed because of greed.

The principle reasons people experience poverty in our country and world are calamity, plague, war, disease, and fraud, over which the victims have no control (Ex. 10:4–5; Num. 11:4–5; Judges 10:8; Psalm 105:34). Jesus commanded the church to "love your neighbor." It is not just a neighborly deed, but a mandate to the church.

Jesus said, "For I was hungry and you gave me something to eat, I was thirsty and you gave me something to drink, I was a stranger and you invited me in, I needed clothes and you clothed me, I was sick and you looked after me, I was in prison and you came to visit me" (Matt. 25:35–36).

SEEKING SOLUTIONS

Westhaven Baptist Church in Memphis, Tennessee, has been very successful with a program designed to train people in computer and data entry skills. Although the church never advertised this program, they received over 100 responses. Memphis representatives of ADIA, an employment placement agency, serve as instructors for the program.

Westhaven also works with other churches in starting "Hope Centers" in multihousing communities. A Hope Center is a church that provides for the spiritual, physical, and emotional needs of the residents through Backyard Bible Clubs and tutorial services for children, group events, worship services, Bible studies, and other specialized ministries.

Every Friday night, Westhaven offers its community a free night at the movies. Located in an area with no theater, the church takes advantage of this opportunity to get the children off the streets by providing a free movie. Westhaven also sponsors the Church Outdoors, a ministry to the homeless that provides a worship service and lunch every Sunday afternoon.

Mendenhall Bible Church in Mendenhall, Mississippi, has established The Mendenhall Ministries. The purpose of the ministry is to develop people and ministries to meet the spiritual and physical needs of the rural poor in Mendenhall, Simpson County, and south central Mississippi, as well as to reach the total human being nationally and worldwide. The ministry serves its nearby communities by providing a variety of ministries including Genesis One Christian School, Christian Youth Leadership Development, Community Law Office, Health Center, a thrift store, a housing ministry, and other programs. Mendenhall Ministries has taken the gospel seriously by meeting many needs for the rural poor.

Calvary Baptist Church of Oak Cliff, located in inner-city Dallas, models a variety of ministries that help combat poverty, including:

- an afterschool ministry to latchkey children, known as Champs.
- Sunset Infant Care for high school mothers who need childcare. This is a joint effort with YMCA.
- Community Outreach Carnival and movie nights.
- three multihousing ministries with children and one with adults.
- an afterschool ministry to at-risk middle schoolers, called Varsity Champs.
- Urban Allies, special projects with other suburban churches doing short-term ministry.
- parenting classes for both churched and nonchurched parents.
- a bus ministry that picks up neighborhood children who otherwise would not be in church. These children also receive a personal visit most weeks to encourage them and remind them of church activities.

Calvary also utilizes summer missions teams sent by suburban churches and sponsors a Thai congregation, two African American congregations, three Hispanic congregations, and one multicultural apartment church.

East Park Baptist Church in Greenville, South Carolina, converted part of its facility for use as a crisis center. Initially, only the members of East Park were involved in this ministry. The ministry continued to grow, however, and today the Eastside Crisis Center is a ministry of the Greenville Baptist Association, utilizing more than 100 volunteers from 20 churches. The center is open four days a week and provides people with food, clothing, and limited financial assistance. Volunteers assisted over 2,100 families during 1995. In every case, they work to give a positive witness for Christ to the people they help.

First Baptist Church in San Antonio, Texas, made an intentional choice to remain in the inner-city. Under the direction of their minister of church and community ministries, the congregation offers:

- a full-service, free dental clinic.
- a volunteer-run, nonprofit restaurant which provides jobs and training for homeless persons and funds the free lunch ministry.
- classes for persons for whom English is a second language; literacy classes in Spanish; and classes in citizenship and for the GED.
- food, clothing, transportation, and shower facilities.
- counseling and accountability through 12-step groups.
- Friendship International for international women and their preschool children.
- chaplaincy at a juvenile detention center.
- recreation and Bible-centered activities at a nearby multi-family housing project.
- volunteers for an interfaith coalition emergency shelter.
- a mentorship program at a local elementary school.

Some Places to Begin

Children and teenagers living in the culture of poverty often turn to drugs and violence as a way not only to escape the cycle but also to acquire income and status. If we ever hope to lessen the violence that plagues our society, we must combat the poverty that often leads to this violence. The Christian community can be instrumental in helping children and teenagers avoid the trap of poverty-provoked violence. Following are some suggestions.

- Pray for a vision for helping others out of poverty.
- Locate and identify the communities your church will target.
- Gather demographic census tracts for these communities.
- Conduct a needs survey of these areas.

•Combat illiteracy by training people to read and write. One out of every five Americans is functionally illiterate, with reading skills below the eighth-grade level.[8]

•Provide basic skill training, and recognize that this is also an effective means through which to teach spiritual and moral values. Lead your church to become a GED center, teach English as a second language, and/or provide tutorial services.

•Involve volunteers in teaching a marketable trade to those who are unemployed. Offer computer classes to teach data entry skills. Follow up with class participants by helping them find a job.

God is at work in our world, even among the poorest of the poor. He calls us to join Him in that work.

Chapter Sixteen

PROMOTE MENTAL WHOLENESS

By Taylor Field

Joe sat in the corner and scowled at the Christian worker who was handing out coffee and cupcakes to the people in the community center. Joe was homeless and troubled, and had become more withdrawn in the last few weeks. He fingered his tattered sleeve and sneered at the young man who was encouraging others as he gave out refreshments.

In a flash, Joe leaped from his seat with the fury of a bull and charged up to the worker serving the coffee. "I'll get you!" Joe exploded and pointed his finger. Everyone in the room stopped and stared. "You're hiding from me the secrets about the three unsaved tribes of Israel! I'll get you for that!" Joe spat out the words in righteous fury as he locked eyes with the puzzled worker.

Joe marched out of the room. Once more the crowd heard him shout from outside, "I'll get you!"

The worker's face flushed crimson. He was embarrassed and hurt. He had been coming simply to give his time at the community center to help those who were having a tough time. He had always been courteous to Joe and had been increasingly puzzled by his bizarre questions about biblical subjects the worker had never heard of. Why he had been singled out for this fury, he did not know. He knew nothing about the three unsaved tribes of Israel. He had not been prepared for this kind of treatment and felt spiritually confused. And scared.

Such treatment is rare in working with people who are troubled or in difficult circumstances, but it occasionally does occur. Volunteers and others who encounter such people regularly need to be prepared by understanding more about those who suffer from mental disorders.

Mental health is that dynamic balance which enables people to accept themselves, to enjoy and care for others, and to meet the demands of life. Mental illness is a term that "describes a broad variety of symptoms that produce distress and/or disability in one's personal, social, or occupational life."[1] When mental health deteriorates, violence can be one kind of behavior out of a broad range of behaviors.

People whose mental health has deteriorated or who have a mental disorder function in a wide range of contexts. Some people who are homeless may be the most obvious examples. It is sad to observe a person on the street who has an unkempt appearance and displays erratic behavior. We may also see people with mental difficulties in assisted care housing or in other mental health programs. Yet there is a vast and complex range of behaviors and experiences that go beyond the dynamic balance in mental health. According to a study by the National Institute of Mental Health, at any given time nearly one out of every five adults suffers from a psychiatric disorder.[2] Of course, the severity of these disorders varies, but we need to be sensitive to the challenges people in our own sphere of activity encounter. We may see the heartbreaking inability to cope even within ourselves, in our own family, in our church, or in our circle of friends and associates. Threatening behavior from someone who is mentally ill can be devastating to a family, church, or ministry.

In my personal experience, I have found violence among those whose mental health has been disrupted to be extremely rare. For over 20 years, I have worked with thousands of homeless people in San Francisco, Hong Kong, and New York who have often exhibited symptoms of mental disorders. Even though I have spent most of my time with people under incredible stress who often have overwhelming emotional, mental, and spiritual needs, I can count on my fingers the number of violent outbursts from them. The possibility of violence should not be one more reason to shun or punish people who are deeply troubled. Yet in order to minister and live in our world, Christians need to be aware of the relationship between violence and mental illness.

BIBLICAL FOUNDATIONS

The Bible is full of the awareness of health in relation to God, of God's constant work in mending the heart, body, and mind. People in the biblical world recognized mental illness as well as mental health. For example, David once pretended to be insane, and his behavior gives us insight into the understanding of mental illness in Old Testament times (1 Sam. 21:13).

Although it is unclear to what some of the terms in the New Testament are referring, Jesus worked in healing a wide range of maladies. Most Christian counselors believe that mental disorders and demon possession refer to different conditions; nevertheless, some of the symptoms are similar. We wince as we read in Mark 5:3–5 about the man who wanders among the tombs and does violence to himself by cutting himself with stones.

What is most helpful for me to study in the Gospels is Jesus' unwillingness to withdraw from those who had been labeled by His society. He did not accept the prevailing views of uncleanness in His day. He did not simply buy in to the labels concerning lepers, the maimed, tax collectors, or even the dead. He reached out with care to everyone He encountered. He saw things differently. Instead of viewing uncleanness as contagious, He saw God's wholeness and goodness as contagious.

In like manner, we need to be careful about destructive labeling. Instead of labeling someone a "wacko" or "nutjob" and using that as an excuse to shun that person, we need to seek to understand and reach out in appropriate ways.

However, in dealing with someone who is potentially violent, we must not be naive. In a different context, Jesus gives instructions that my coworkers and I often use in our ministry when we work with deeply troubled people in the inner-city. "Therefore be as shrewd as snakes and as innocent as doves" (Matt. 10:16b). We are to be both aware and wise as we encounter new people and situations.

I often remind myself, "I am not the Savior." I cannot save or rescue anyone. When dealing with someone who is potentially disruptive, my colleagues and I always go in pairs, and are careful not to have a "Savior complex." We do not try to rush in and thus set ourselves up in a dangerous situation.

In one sense, the church is rediscovering its rightful gentle power in dealing with mental health and mental illness. In our world, those who are professionally trained must make evaluations about an individual's ability to cope. Yet the church has great opportunities in providing understanding and patience and in bringing together a group who will walk through difficulties with someone who is deeply troubled.

In the 1980s, many individuals and churches became aware of the problems of those who were mentally ill. Churches began to reach out to the homeless by providing meals or shelter. Through these encounters, God continues to stir the hearts of Christian believers. Some have grown in the special qualities of kindness, patience, and firmness that enable them to minister to people with disturbing behaviors.

Other churches have worked with mental health programs in their communities to provide friendship and support groups. Such experiences have opened the eyes of many to the power of a God-given tenacity and love in transcending seemingly insuperable barriers.

The simple things may prove to be most effective in helping with violent behavior and mental illness. Churches have provided invaluable help to families that are dealing with a family member who behaves violently or erratically. I frequently hear, "We could never have made it through that difficult time without our church." Stories of heroism abound which illustrate how a local church stood by a fellow Christian as that person recovered from violent behavior and mental illness.

God has commanded us to love everyone. However, each of us has a choice in deciding if we will be obedient and love others or disobedient and ignore others. Some groups or churches have chosen to ignore individuals or families in deep need because people simply don't know what to do or are frightened. Yet other churches have seized the opportunity to sensitize their own congregation and the community by offering seminars or training sessions which help alleviate fears concerning mental illness. The networking that churches have done with Christian counselors and other professionals has helped break the barriers of ignorance.

SEEKING SOLUTIONS

Some of the most effective work has come from people trying to deal with their own heartbreak. Jack and Jo Ann Hinckley went through a nightmare of anguish as they tried to understand why two of their children were outstanding leaders and another tried to assassinate the President of the United States, Ronald Reagan. Instead of retiring into their own anguish, this couple established the American Mental Health Fund to support research and to provide public education about mental illness. They are dedicated to preventing mental disorders so that other families can be spared the tragedy they have endured.[3]

Without making it their primary focus, other ministries and individuals work to help prevent mental disorders and violence. Mental health involves so many factors. As Christians and churches work to alleviate stressful living in the inner-city, alleviate family disorders, or provide opportunities for decent employment, they may assist in preventing serious mental illness and violence.

Following are some things you can do to promote mental health in your community:

Take a personal interest and get involved. By finding out about the mental health programs and facilities in your community, you can take a step toward understanding the unique challenges concerning mental health. As you make phone calls and ask questions, you will encounter professionals who work with these issues every day and who may provide valuable insight. The opportunity may arise to work in a mental health program or to get involved with a ministry with people who are homeless.

Be sensitive to those who may be struggling with mental health in your own church. As you watch and listen, you may become more aware of those who are struggling with violence and mental illness. The clearer window into the awesome loneliness and anguish of mental illness is a humbling experience.

Most of us are not in a position to determine if someone is mentally ill. That determination is a medical responsibility. However, we can be aware of symptoms that may indicate mental illness or other trouble: a change in behavior, a change in general appearance, distorted communication, increasing suspicion of people, indications of violence, explosive behavior.

When confronting violence stemming from mental illness, we must be quick to recognize when we are in over our heads. We need to be aware of good sense and know when to get more experienced people involved in a problem. Our poor Christian worker who had trouble with Joe at the beginning of this chapter needs some help from others. It is important to be aware of the treatment sources in our own communities and to be able to call others when we become uncomfortable. Ignoring violent behavior is certainly not helpful for the person engaging in it, and in rare instances, it may be dangerous for us as well as others.

Encourage your church to provide educational opportunities concerning mental health and violence. A little information and insight from people with experience or from trained professionals can open new horizons of understanding human beings with distinctive difficulties.

When we become more sensitive to symptoms of mental illness, know who to turn to in times of need, and encourage education, we take steps toward a more Christlike care for those in deep trouble.

Some Underlying Principles

I have found the following concepts to be helpful in working with people whose mental health may be deteriorating and who may be potentially disruptive. I do not speak as a trained professional, but simply as a minister who works in community services in the inner-city. Because of the nature of our work and our neighborhood, we encounter people who may be labeled as runaways, heroin addicts, anarchists, alcoholics, squatters, crackheads, or skinheads. In planning for the future, the element of choice for some seems very small. For me, however, the ones who seem to be mentally ill are the most trapped by their situation and have the fewest choices as they wander from place to place, haunted by their own extreme limitations. Following are some simple things I have learned as I have related to people in such challenging circumstances:

• *The value of unceasing prayer (1 Thess. 5:17)*. It is essential to cultivate the undercurrent of prayer as we engage in the day-to-day requirements of walking beside people in trouble. In threatening or disorienting circumstances, we often sense that we are engaging forces beyond our comprehension. The value of quietly acknowledging God's power and presence in intense situations seems more and more important to me as I grow older. During such trying interaction, Paul's instruction to pray at all times seems especially appropriate.

• *The power of the risen Christ.* I sometimes find myself praying that everything I hear and say will be filtered through the self-giving love of Christ Who stands among us. Sometimes I pray that the gentle Spirit of Christ will envelop and fill the person with whom I am talking.

• *The need for discernment, which results in knowing what to say or to do.* If no discernment comes, hard-nosed patience, attention, and understanding need to prevail. With greater understanding, my coworkers and I have grown to accept the fact that we may not receive responses that come in a normal fashion. We do not try to argue with someone who appears to be deeply disturbed. We can often listen behind the words to hear the deeper longings of an individual. Spiritual questions and yearnings need to be handled with care and respect.

• *Wisdom in knowing when to assist the conflicting parties in disruptive circumstances in getting some space from each other.* In some areas, where few people know each other, calling the troubled person by name and inviting him or her to come outside in the open air may be helpful. Sometimes (but not always) allowing someone to talk out some of the frustrations may prove calming. The old dictum, "Talk it out; don't act it out," is often a good principle. Humor sometimes is a saving grace. Recently a gentleman who had been in and out of mental hospitals much of his life and presently shoulders his worldly possessions on his back looked at me with a twinkle in his eye. "The best thing about losing it all," he said with a wry smile, "is you don't have to carry it with you."

• *The importance of encouraging people to seek further treatment and find ways to deal constructively with their mental health issues.* Such encouragement can be important in alleviating stress and minimizing the chance of a tailspin into violent behavior.

• *The value of common sense.* By their very nature, encounters with people struggling with mental health can be unpredictable, and holy good sense is important. Depending on people with more experience or more professional training is essential.

• *The necessity for advocacy.* As our understanding and empathy increase, we have the opportunity to be advocates in our churches and communities for better attention for those whose mental health is challenged and who are potentially disruptive. Support and education may emerge in your own church, and the possibility of developing a working relationship with other community mental health programs increases. Such active involvement can help one of the most maligned and least understood parts of our population.

I do not believe that God has called everyone to work with those who have mental health challenges and to face the accompanying possibility of violence. God will stir up those with the firmness, kindness, and good sense to face the task. But when we do encounter the kinds of troubles the Christian worker faced at the beginning of the chapter, we do not need to remain alone or confused. As we learn more, we receive the constant reminder of the fragility of our human existence by glimpsing the suffering of others.

If the earthly Jesus were here today, where would He go? Certainly not in the most comfortable spot, or the most protected place, or the place where He felt most secure. He would be with those who are most sick and who are least able to handle things on their own. He still calls us to follow Him there.

Chapter Seventeen

LESSEN THE LIKELIHOOD OF SUICIDE

By Sandy Wisdom-Martin

This is the dispatcher. We need your help. A 16-year-old has committed suicide."

The phone call breaks the silence of an early winter morning. The unthinkable strikes an unsuspecting family. A vibrant youth with endless potential could not see past the heartbreak of the moment. Hearing a noise in the driveway, his mother looked at the front door and saw her son behind the wheel of the car, warming the engine. He mouthed the words, "I'm sorry, Mom," as he drove away. The police caught up with him in front of his ex-girlfriend's house. As officers approached the car, he put a revolver to his head and pulled the trigger.

This is not an isolated incident in American life. It represents a growing epidemic. On an average day, 84 people die from suicide and an estimated 1,900 adults attempt suicide.[1] Many experts believe this is a conservative figure. Because suicide carries such a stigma, relatives often assign other causes of death, such as automobile accidents or drug overdoses. Survivors are left to work through denial, shock, pain, shame, guilt, anger, and helplessness.

Many myths surround suicide. Some of the most commonly cited misconceptions include the following:[2]

140

Myth 1: People who talk about (or threaten) suicide don't really mean it. This myth is one of the most widely believed and potentially dangerous. Alan L. Berman, former president of the American Association of Suicidology, says, "Anyone who threatens suicide should be taken seriously. Approximately three-fourths of people who attempt suicide have given prior messages." A suicide threat is a cry for help. It is better to respond to the threat than to risk the loss of a life.

Myth 2: Once a person is suicidal, he or she is suicidal forever. Most people are suicidal for a limited amount of time. If a person receives appropriate help, he or she is often able to move beyond the immediate threat of suicide. Nine out of ten people who attempt suicide never try again.

Myth 3: Suicidal people always leave a suicide note. Less than one-fourth of those who commit suicide leave a suicide note. This popular myth is one reason why friends and family members often refuse to accept the fact that their loved one has committed suicide.

Myth 4: Women threaten suicide, while men actually go through with it. While it is true that more men than women kill themselves, one cannot discount the sincerity of a woman's suicide threat. Women are four times more likely to attempt suicide than men. Women often try unsuccessful suicide approaches such as pills or carbon monoxide poisoning. Men use direct methods such as shooting or hanging.

Myth 5: Those who commit suicide are insane. A suicidal person may not be completely rational. The individual may not be responsible for his or her act. However, this does not mean the person is insane.

Myth 6: Religious people are less likely to commit suicide. People from all different religious faiths and belief systems commit suicide.

BIBLICAL FOUNDATIONS

Read Matthew 7:24–27. In these and the surrounding verses known as the Beatitudes, Jesus tells people how to live life. He ends with this story of the two foundations. The first man builds his house on the rock, which Jesus compares to those who hear His teachings and act on them. The second man builds his house on the sand, which He compares to those who hear but do not act on His words.

Our world offers many different teachings on how to live. It promises that we will find happiness in possessions, fame, and relationships. Luke's account of this story tells us that the man who built his house on the rock dug deeply. He did not take any shortcuts, but worked diligently to make sure his house was stable. Those who base their lives on the shifting sands of this world's teachings take a dangerous shortcut. Those who desire stable lives wisely base them on the solid rock of Jesus' teaching.

Wise people also plan and prepare ahead. Life will assuredly bring storms. Yet when storms come, most people are surprised and unprepared. During the calm times of life, when the storms are nowhere around, those who are wise prepare for those storms that will surely one day come. By digging deeply into the teachings of God's Word and firmly planting their lives there, they build a solid foundation. When tragedies come, their foundation holds because of the truths of Christ's teachings.

Only in God's Word will people find answers to the basic questions of life. As we read and study God's Word, we can discover how God wants us to spend our lives. When we build our lives on Jesus' teachings, the storms of life may destroy all we have, but they will not destroy our lives. When we base our lives on the shifting sand of this world's teachings, the fall of our lives will be great.

Many people who attempt suicide have heard the words of Jesus, but have not acted on them. When the storms of life come, they sink in the shifting sands.

As you think about how you and your church can decrease the violence of suicide and attempted suicide, consider these questions:

- What are some storms of life you and your family members have faced (i.e., loss of job, loss of home or possessions, loss of a close friend or family member, a terminal diagnosis)?
- How did you choose to handle those storms?
- What are some ways you can prepare yourself for other storms life will bring?
- What are some practical ways to help others through their storms of life?
- Where is God in the storms of life?

SEEKING SOLUTIONS

Bud and Peggy Daven were proud grandparents of a precious one-week-old baby when their world turned upside down. Their daughter, suffering from postpartum psychosis, committed suicide in their home. Bud and Peggy used their experience with this sudden death to help bring healing to other families. Together they started a Survivors of Suicide (SOS) group in their community.

SOS is a volunteer support group that meets monthly. Membership is open to anyone who has lost a family member to suicide. Bud says, "You can gain strength as you listen to others who have experienced the same thing you have." Bud and Peggy have since helped begin SOS organizations in other communities in their state. Their goal is to provide support groups within one hour of anyone who needs one.

When crisis comes to one of the 208 schools within the Dallas public school system, faculty and staff are prepared to respond. In the late 1980s, school officials worked with community mental health professionals to develop policies and procedures to deal with suicide prevention, intervention, and follow-up. Special classroom curriculum helps children develop coping skills and learn how to help peers who are suicidal. Seminars, group work, parenting programs, and counseling help implement other prevention techniques. Faculty and staff learn warning signs for suicide. School counselors, social workers, and school psychologists receive intensive training on risk assessment and intervention techniques. After a suicide, a crisis team helps the school deal with the crisis. Part of this work is to identify at-risk children to prevent more suicides. If your school does not have a suicide prevention/intervention program in place, consider getting information about the Dallas school-based program.[3]

Some Places to Begin

Following are ways you can help reduce the likelihood of suicide in your community:

1. Get information from the local library, community mental health counseling centers, hospital chaplains, social workers, and other resources. Suicide is a complicated topic. Learn all you can about the subject. Begin here by considering these answers to some frequently asked questions about suicide.[4]

Why do people commit suicide? Many people who commit suicide have overwhelming feelings of hopelessness and helplessness. They do not see any other way out of their current situation.

How can one help a person who is suicidal? A suicidal person often feels worthless and unloved. As you care, listen, and support a suicidal person, you help that individual understand that life may be worth living.

How can talking about suicide help prevent it? Talking about suicide helps diffuse some of the feelings of hopelessness and helplessness. It helps the person connect to desperately needed available help, creating a climate of caring and helping break through loneliness the person is experiencing.

Is it true that people who attempt to kill themselves really don't want to die? Most people who commit suicide are ambivalent about whether to live or die right up to the moment of death. They want to live and die at the same time.

Why do some people keep suicide a family secret? Some

people fear what others will think and say. They are afraid of being blamed and ostracized. It seems, however, much of the stigma of suicide is lifting. People are more willing to deal with suicide openly and honestly now than in previous years.

Does everyone think about committing suicide at least once in his or her lifetime? Most people will have fleeting thoughts of suicide at some point in their lives.

2. Know your limits. Do not get in over your head when dealing with a suicidal individual. Be willing to make a referral to a person who is in a better situation to help.

3. Identify resources available in your community before a crisis occurs. Locate mental health professionals who can provide assistance as a preventive measure or in a crisis situation. Before enlisting assistance, review their qualifications. Make sure the professional is trained in crisis intervention and experienced in dealing with suicide. Ask about their availability during times of crisis. Make sure the individual has appropriate certification and licensure from their state. Here is a list of helping professionals to consider.[5]

Psychiatrist: A medical doctor who also has training in treating mental and emotional illnesses. A psychiatrist and a medical doctor can prescribe drugs to treat depression and mental disorders.

Licensed Psychologist: A trained professional who can provide evaluation and treatment of mental disorders. This professional must have a PhD, EdD, or PsyD degree plus several years of supervised clinical experience.

Clinical Social Worker: A master's-level, trained practitioner who helps individuals, families, and groups increase their capacity for solving problems. A social worker can provide counseling, help people increase their coping skills, and locate available resources.

Licensed Professional Counselor or Therapist: An individual who has a master's or doctoral degree in marriage/family, child counseling, counseling, or psychology.

Psychiatric Nurse Clinician: A registered nurse who has at least a master's degree in mental health nursing and supervised experience in working with emotionally distressed individuals.

4. Learn to recognize signs of suicidal behavior. Rita Robinson suggests the following as warning signs:[6]
•Suicide threats
•Previous suicide attempts
•Statements revealing a desire to die
•A preoccupation with death
•Giving away personal effects and getting affairs in order
•Personality changes or odd behavior
•Withdrawal, apathy, moodiness, anger, sleeplessness, depression
•Loss of appetite
•Statements about hopelessness, helplessness, or worthlessness
•Isolating self from others
•Loss of interest in usual activities
•Sudden appearance of happiness and calmness

If someone exhibits these signs, *act*. Do not promise to keep information confidential if someone tells you they are thinking about committing suicide.

5. Work with school officials, mental health professionals, and other community organizations to develop an appropriate prevention, intervention, and postvention strategy for your public school system.

6. Start a support group for suicide survivors or allow a support group to use your church facility for meetings.

7. Ask a mental health professional to come to your church to provide suicide education.

8. Minister to suicide survivors.
•Do not say, "Please call if I can help." The call will never

come. Grieving individuals are overwhelmed. Suggest things you are ready and willing to do.

• Visit the bereaved. Many times friends abandon survivors of suicide because they do not know what to say or do. Your presence shows you care.

• Let them talk. They need to verbalize their feelings and frustrations. They usually do not want advice. Allow them to share about the loved one they have lost.

• Provide food. It is best to send food already cooked.

• Provide ongoing support by phone. Send cards and letters. Remember to make a special effort on holidays and anniversaries of the death.

• Provide child care.

• Provide assistance with household chores and yard work.

• Keep a list of phone calls, visitors, and people who bring food.

• Do not tell the person you know how they feel if you don't.

• Do not preach. The individual will draw strength from God when they need it. Do not tell them it is God's will.

9. Organize community workshops on grief, specifically gearing them toward helping someone cope with a loss or preparing people for times when they will face grief. Be sure to carefully select workshop leaders who are trained and experienced in working with grief recovery. Check local hospital chaplains or hospice social workers to get input and suggestions.

10. Give witness to the Christian faith. In times of crisis, people are often more receptive to the gospel of Christ. They realize circumstances of life are beyond their control and are willing to put their trust in God. Being a Christian example of love and service during a time of crisis will provide a strong witness to grieving individuals. You can also provide a verbal witness. Be sensitive to the person's emotional condition. Do not argue or preach. Simply share the good news that God loves and cares for them. When it is appropriate, talk with them about how to become a Christian.

Chapter Eighteen

WORK WITHIN THE CRIMINAL JUSTICE SYSTEM

By Jack Poe

The phrase *criminal justice system* elicits many different reactions. Some call it the *criminals' justice system*; some refer to it as the *criminal injustice system*. The true picture of America's criminal justice system is somewhere in the middle.

Certain concepts within the criminal justice system ensure that it provides fair and impartial treatment for those who need its services. The Constitution of the United States guarantees fair treatment to everyone accused of violating the law. Justice is a vital, complicated, and essential part of the criminal justice system. The process must not just *appear* fair; it must *be* fair. Fairness is the cornerstone of a free and humane society.

The criminal justice system provides impartial treatment when the law enforcement community, the court system, and the correctional agencies are equal players. Each of these components has broad discretionary powers. Each serves a specific purpose within the system. Each devotes time, effort, and professionalism to its discipline to ensure its tasks are performed with utmost effectiveness.

The law enforcement community is the first component that initiates contact with the public in the criminal justice system. It entrusts law enforcement officers with a great deal of discretionary power. A law enforcement officer can, with probable cause, detain another member of society. The interpretation of the law and the public's perception of the law meet first with the officer on the street. "The police officer thus becomes the first 'interpreter' of the law in the criminal justice process; the person who carries this enormous responsibility must both recognize and be continually reminded of the fact that he or she stands under the law which is his or her responsibility to interpret and enforce."[1]

Law enforcement officers take this responsibility seriously. Their fidelity to this principle is steadfast. Their training in the use of force is ongoing. They know their actions on the street, often performed in extreme and stressful situations, will be judged by their supervisory officers, the public prosecutor, the defense counsel, and the public. This review of their actions will be conducted after the fact, with the luxury of time for reflection that most often the officer did not have.

The court system is the next component that plays an important part in the criminal justice process. In the words of Justice Arthur T. Vanderbilt:

> It is in the courts and not in the legislature that our citizens primarily feel the keen cutting edge of the law. If they have respect for the work of the courts, their respect for law will survive the shortcomings of every other branch of government, but if they lose their respect for the work of the courts, their respect for law and order will vanish with it to the great detriment of society.[2]

Today, maybe even more so than in days past, society looks to the courts for relief, restitution, and adjudication of crime in our country.

Members of a society have the right to a speedy determination of guilt or innocence along with proper legal representation. In 1960, the United States Supreme Court handed down some monumental decisions that changed the way officers enforced the law. The decisions gave citizens the right to legal counsel even when they could not afford it, and the right of counsel to prevent self-incrimination.[3] This process has produced an adversarial climate between the agencies that make up the criminal justice system. Some argue that this is necessary to keep the relationship between police, prosecutors, courts, and corrections distant. Too cozy a relationship would destroy the justice in the criminal justice system.[4]

The third component of the criminal justice system includes corrections, pardon, and parole. Prisons, halfway houses, community-based corrections, and detention centers serve to incarcerate. The pardon and parole sections give supervision to those released from incarceration who still have time left to serve on their sentences.

Prisons and detention centers have few voluntary residents. Dissatisfaction with them is universal. Too often they are breeding grounds for brutality, violence, and racial confrontation. Gangs inside the walls of many correctional institutions are more violent than their counterparts outside. Mistrust, misconduct, and injustice rule the day. Correctional administrators and staff charged with providing protective custody often do so with fear for their own safety.

Punishment for serious crimes by imprisonment is an American invention which began in the early eighteenth century.[5] Early leaders saw it as a way to cure criminal behavior. Evidence from the last two centuries indicates that this rehabilitative process has failed. Criminal behavior is at an all-time high.[6] We cannot build prisons fast enough to meet the demands of the court. Frustrated citizens are demanding truth in sentencing laws and mandated sectioning for repeat offenders.

Victims' rights groups are increasing and related legislation is in effect nationally. The National Association of Victim Assistance has become a part of the Department of Justice, and most district attorneys have assigned specific individuals to work with victims who come through their jurisdiction.

Sometimes the forgotten factor in the lives of those incarcerated is their families. Spouses and children constitute a large but often neglected segment of victims affected by crime. It is important that a formal network be set up to maintain, as much as possible, the ties between the inmate and the inmate's family. The closeness of the prisoner's family is a good indicator of whether he or she will be rehabilitated and integrated back into society.

Sociologists teach us that if there are no effective community social controls at work, there is little law enforcement agencies can do to deal with crime.[7] Social control comes from the community itself. What the criminal justice system deals with, then, can be seen as the product of the public's own decisions. Processes are in place to include citizens in the criminal justice system: Citizens elect public officials, serve on policy boards and legislative committees, and establish statutes and ordinances that become law.

The criminal justice system is only as effective as the community is involved. Community in America is at a crossroads between guarding individual civil rights and protecting itself against the tremendous increase in crime. A renewed commitment between the criminal justice system and citizens may be a good place to start. Most Americans are concerned with the problems of our criminal justice system and are willing to become proactive in finding solutions.

BIBLICAL FOUNDATIONS

Read Luke 10:30–37. On the Jericho roads of life people are beaten and left for dead. They ask, "Is there a God, and if there is, does He really care?" The only way many of them will ever know is if God's children take time to touch a life and make a difference.

The parable of the good Samaritan defines the nature of the campaign Jesus undertook on His journey to Jerusalem. He, like the Samaritan, was on a business journey and was in a hurry to fulfill His mission.

Like the Samaritan, He was delayed by His compassion for the lost, sick, hurting, and dying, all of whom were victims of the world's carelessness and cruelty. Neither the priest nor the Levite took time to help in the parable of the good Samaritan. But our Lord could not pass us by, and while He lingered was Himself overtaken.

He has entrusted His work to us. As He proved Himself our neighbor at such a great cost, we also we must prove ourselves neighbors in a world rapidly becoming as hostile to our faith as it was to Him.

The question is not *Who is my neighbor?* but *To whom can I show myself a neighbor?* Jesus Himself was nicknamed a Samaritan (John 8:48). The scholars may have been correct when they suggested that Jesus was thinking of His journey along the dangerous road of life. Jesus, in the parable of the good Samaritan, expanded the word *neighbor* to include not only the Jews, but every child of the human race, however lowly and despised. To Jesus, a neighbor is anyone who needs help. Likewise, anyone who renders help is neighborly.

Willingness to suffer and engage in sacrificial service, not ambition for high places, is essential for those who wish to be part of the kingdom of God. The life of Christ is an example of dedication and determination. His life was consumed by burning compassion to help others. Jesus said the measure of our greatness in God's kingdom is our servanthood. But a servant attitude—doing simple acts for others—does not come easily. We develop the spirit of servanthood not by lordship over others, but by engaging in devoted service to them. Jesus points to His own life as an example of servanthood: "Just as the Son of Man did not come to be served, but to serve, and to give His life a ransom for many" (Matt. 20:28). God chooses people for great service in the kingdom of God, but chosen people must prove themselves worthy. People do not care how much we know until they know how much we care.

Scripture commands that we get involved with others. Helping often involves our own area of expertise. This may involve making small household repairs, sewing, cooking, or taking others to shop or to the doctor's office. Being involved with others' needs always makes us aware of our obligation to pray for their needs. Caring enough to serve fulfills the law of Christ (Gal. 6:2).

SEEKING SOLUTIONS

... Within the Law Enforcement Community

Adopt-a-Cop. Select an officer by name for whom you will pray daily. Find out his or her birthday and send a card to the department to remind the officer of your prayers. Some churches have enacted this program under the name Shield a Badge.

Host a Law Enforcement Recognition Day. Every year in May, local law enforcement departments honor their officers killed in the line of duty. These activities coincide with activities held in Washington, DC, on May 15 honoring all officers killed in the line of duty during the past year. Establish a Law Enforcement Recognition Day in your area. Invite local officers to take part in the service by leading in prayer, reading a Scripture, giving their testimony, singing, or speaking.

Resource the local chaplain. If your local police department has a chaplain, contact him or her and ask what you can do to help resource their program. Supply birthday, sympathy, get well, or other cards. Or provide stamps, counseling books, or other material for the officers.

Provide special recognition. Have a "reverse citation" program. Print up some reverse citation certifications with your church's name on them. When you know of an officer who has done an exceptional job, write a citation and send it to the chief of police with the officer's name and accomplishment on it.

... Within the Courts

For the most part, representatives from the church community appear in court to offer support, comfort, and assistance to the accused. Victims of crime and violent acts also need this support from the Christian community.

Participate in court watch. Go to trial and give support to the accused and his or her family members, *or* go to the trial and give support to the victim and the victim's family members. (You cannot give support to the accused and the victim at the same time.)

Become proactive in crime prevention. Contact the local sheriff and/or police chief to see if they have signed a TRIAD agreement. TRIAD is an agreement between the local sheriff's department, police department, and chapter of the American Association of Retired Persons. Out of this agreement a SALT council usually forms. SALT stands for Seniors and Law Enforcement Together. SALT councils around the country have already developed many programs for senior adults to help combat and prevent violence. There is no need to reinvent the wheel. Contact your local SALT council and get involved.

Start support groups. Many support groups already exist, but your church can form its own chapter and provide spiritual input into the healing process for victims. Contact the victim assistance coordinator at your local district attorney's office for the contact for such groups as The Compassionate Friends, Mothers Against Drunk Driving, Survivors of Homicide Victims, and domestic violence support groups. NOVA, the National Organization for Victim Assistance in Washington, DC, is another valuable source of information and training.

. . . Within Corrections and Parole

The ever-increasing number of people in penal institutions is a field unto harvest in itself. Hearing the words, "Stop this behavior or spend the rest of your life in prison," can become the sobering moment when an individual realizes that the gospel is his or her only hope to change. Ministers and lay leaders can serve as volunteer chaplains to help those individuals come to know Jesus Christ.

Determine the need and establish an associational missions development program. Contact the state chaplaincy director for help and suggestions.

Train volunteers who have a deep concern for individuals and who are dependable and teachable.

Plan a one-day workshop or seminar for those interested in volunteering. Ask the warden, sheriff, or jailer to speak on the rules of the jail or prison. Enlist the prison chaplain to speak on the role of the volunteer chaplain.

Provide special programs such as visiting speakers, music groups, and seasonal programs.

Establish a hospitality house where inmates' families can stay while visiting inmates at the correctional institution. This is an especially great need in areas with few hotels. Many times the families do not have enough money for a hotel even if one is available. They often live out of their cars until they return home.

When an inmate is getting ready to return home, a church can sponsor the inmate and his or her family. The church can help the family as they prepare for their loved one's return. They can help the inmate find employment, help the family find a place to live, and above all, they can help the family reintegrate into society. The church's faith in the inmate may be just the key he or she needs to become a productive member of society.

RESOURCES FOR FURTHER HELP

Chapter One—Promote Peace in Families

Dockrey, Karen. *Growing a Family Where People Really Like Each Other.* Minneapolis, MN: Bethany, 1996.

Chapter Two—Promote Peace in Communities

Bolton, Joy. *Ideas for Community Ministries.* Birmingham: Woman's Missionary Union, 1993. Call 1-800-968-7301 to order.

Chapter Three—Extend the Walls of the Church

Brown, Robert McAfee, and Sydney Thomson Brown, eds. *A Cry For Justice: The Churches and Synagogues Speak.* New York: Paulist Press, 1989.

Donaghy, John A. *Peacemaking and the Community of Faith: A Handbook for Congregations.* New Jersey: Paulist Press, 1983.

Chapter Four—Care for, Love, and Protect Children

Organizations

The Center for the Prevention of Sexual and Domestic Violence
936 N. 34th Street, Suite 200
Seattle, WA 98103
(206) 634-1903
www.cpsdv.org

The Center for the Prevention of Sexual and Domestic Violence is an inter-religious, educational ministry that assists faith communities in responding to violence. CPSDV offers print and video resources, including curricula entitled *Preventing Child Abuse*, for teachers of children aged five through teens. These curricula are designed for a Christian education setting. Videos include *Hear Their Cries: Religious Responses to Child Abuse* and *Bless Our Children: Preventing Sexual Abuse*; both are excellent for training workshops and increasing awareness of abuse. Other powerful videos addressing domestic violence and clergy misconduct are also available.

The Southern Baptist child advocacy group is:
Child Advocacy Network (CAN)
Attention: Barbara Massey
Woman's Missionary Union
P. O. Box 830010
Birmingham, AL 35283-0010
(205) 991-4057
Meets annually to discuss child advocacy issues, share resources, and promote projects.

Child Welfare League of America
440 First Street, NW, Third Floor
Washington, DC 20001-2085
(202) 638-2952

National Association of Homes for Children
1701 K Street, NW, Suite 200
Washington, DC 20006-1503
(202) 223-3447
The two above organizations can direct you to a local child welfare agency where you may become involved.

Children's Defense Fund (CDF)
25 E Street, NW
Washington, DC 20001
(202) 628-8787
www.childrensdefense.org

Children's Defense Fund has numerous resources essential to anyone committed to addressing the needs of children, with many resources related to violence. Particularly pertinent departments include Religious Affairs Division, Violence Prevention, and Child Welfare Division.

Resources include: *The State of America's Children*, a yearbook that gives data, state-by-state, regarding the status of children in various areas; and *Welcome the Child* (manual and/or video), a practical and comprehensive tool for any church wanting to begin or strengthen efforts to help children.

The National Observance of Children's Sabbath is held the third Sunday of each October. CDF supplies books on the National Observance of Children's Sabbath that provide planning tips, worship resources, and activity ideas for interested Protestant, Catholic, and Jewish organizations.

National Committee for the Prevention of Child Abuse
332 South Michigan Avenue, Suite 1600
Chicago, IL 60604
(312) 663-3520
Supplies information and free materials on parental stress and child abuse.

Books and Curricula

Garland, Diana. *Precious in His Sight: A Guide to Child Advocacy.* 3rd ed. Birmingham, AL: New Hope, 1997.
Gives compact, comprehensive, and practical information and advice on how to advocate and intervene on behalf of children.

Reducing the Risk of Child Sexual Abuse in the Church
Prevention Kit
Christian Ministry Resources
P. O. Box 1098
Matthews, NC 28106
1-800-222-1840

Offers a guidebook that provides resources for churches to develop policies, procedures, and programs for preventing child sexual abuse in the church.

Violence: A Christian Response, coordinated by Phil Strickland and Oeita Borrorff. Published jointly by the Cooperative Baptist Fellowship and the Christian Life Commission of the Baptist General Convention of Texas. To order, call 1-888-801-4223.

Addresses multiple levels of violence. Can be used in various forums, such as elective Sunday School lessons or workshops. Particularly pertinent to the topic of children and violence are the sections on understanding child abuse; programs addressing child abuse; legal issues for churches regarding child abuse; and guidelines for church workers to recognize abuse.

Clinton, Hillary Rodham. *It Takes a Village: And Other Lessons Our Children Teach Us.* New York: Simon and Schuster, 1996.

Pipher, Mary. *The Shelter of Each Other: Rebuilding Our Families.* New York, NY: Grosset/Putnam Book, 1996.

Chapter Five —Nurture and Equip Youth

Organizations

Children's Defense Fund
25 E Street NW
Washington, DC 20001
(202) 628-8787

Children's Welfare League of America
440 First Street NW, Third Floor
Washington, DC 20001-2085
(202) 638-2952

Juvenile Justice Clearinghouse
Send inquiries to:
NCJRS
P. O. Box 6000
Rockville, MD 20849-6000
1-800-638-8736

Centers for Disease Control and Prevention
1600 Clifton Road
Atlanta, GA 30333
(404) 639-3311

Books and Curricula

Violence: A Christian Response, coordinated by Phil Strickland
and Oeita Borrorff. (Published jointly by the Cooperative
Baptist Fellowship and the Christian Life Commission of
the Baptist General Convention of Texas.) To order, call
1-888-801-4223.

Dodd, Charlie, and Jimmy Myers, comps. *Violence: The Desensitized Generation.* Nashville: Convention Press, 1994. A
13-week Bible study for youth with reproducible work
sheets. To order, call 1-800-458-2772. Ask for item #07-
673-197-29.

New Mexico Center for Dispute Resolution. *Violence Intervention Curriculum for Families.* Albuquerque, NM: New
Mexico Center for Dispute Resolution, 1996.

———. *Violence Intervention Curriculum for Juveniles.* Albuquerque, NM: New Mexico Center for Dispute Resolution,
1996.

The two above materials for youth and parents focus on communication and conflict resolution skills, conflict
management, consequential thinking, and problem solving.
The curriculum integrates a number of experiential activities.

Smith, Melinda, ed. *Mediation and Conflict Resolution for Gang-Involved Youth: A Training and Resource Manual.* Albuquerque, NM: New Mexico Center for Dispute Resolution, 1990. Training provided by organization.

Chapter Six—Diminish the Lure of Gangs

Books and Curricula

Gang Ministry Manual (632-35P)
North American Mission Board
4200 North Point Parkway
Alpharetta, GA 30022-4176
1-800-233-1123

Reaching the Cities—Teleconference Video
Children/Youth in Crisis: Gangs
North American Mission Board
4200 North Point Parkway
Alpharetta, GA 30022-4176
Contact: Jane Bishop
(770) 410-6465

Ain't No Denying: Gangs in the 90's
Living Hope Press
600 S. McKinley, Suite 403
Little Rock, AR 72205
1-888-800-HOPE (4673)

Organizations

Your local middle school and high school are good resources. Based on what you learn, you may need to contact the local elementary school.

Another good resource is your local sheriff's or police department. Ask about GREAT (Gang Resistance Education Training Program) developed through the Bureau of Alcohol,

Tobacco and Firearms and the Phoenix Police Department. Now a national training program taught by uniformed officers (1-800-726-7070).

Chapter Seven—Cultivate Domestic Harmony

Wallis, Jim. *The Soul of Politics*. San Diego: Harcourt Brace & Company, 1995.

"Beginning a Ministry with Victims of Domestic Violence" (632-79F). To order from North American Mission Board Customer Services, call 1-800-634-2462.

Chapter Eight—Respect Your Elders

Alzheimer's Association
919 N. Michigan Avenue, Suite 1000
Chicago, IL 60611-1676
1-800-272-3900

American Association of Retired Persons
601 E Street, NW
Washington, DC 20049
(202) 434-2277
Call to request materials on abuse and neglect of the elderly.

National Center on Elder Abuse
810 First Street, NE, Suite 500
Washington, DC 20002
(202) 682-2470

National Family Caregivers Association
9621 E. Bexhill Drive
Kensington, MD 20895-3104
(301) 942-6430

Chapter Nine—Build Bridges of Love

Ford, Clyde W. *We* Can *All Get Along: 50 Steps You Can Take to Help End Racism.* New York: Dell Publishing, 1994.

Harvey, Carol, and M. June Allard. *Understanding Diversity.* New York: HarperCollins College Publishers, 1995.

Kohls, Robert L., and John M. Knight. *Developing Intercultural Awareness: A Cross Cultural Training Handbook.* 2nd ed. Yarmouth, ME: Intercultural Press, 1994.

Clay, Ele, ed. *Many Nations Under God.* Birmingham, AL: New Hope, 1997.

Chapter Ten—The Unspeakable Crime

Books and Curricula

Bass, Ellen, and Laura Davis. *The Courage to Heal: A Guide for Women Survivors of Child Sexual Abuse.* New York: Perennial Library, 1988.

Bass, Ellen, and Louise Thornton. *I Never Told Anyone: Writing by Women of Child Sexual Abuse.* New York: Harper & Row, 1983.

Organizations

Children of the Night
P. O. Box 4343
Hollywood, CA 90078
1-800-551-1300

National Center for Missing and Exploited Children
2101 Wilson Boulevard, Suite 550
Arlington, VA 22201
1-800-843-5678

9 to 5 Job Problems Hotline. Call 1-800-522-0925 to learn how to file a sexual harassment complaint.

RAINN (Rape Abuse and Incest National Network.) Call 1-800-656-4673 to locate a rape crisis center near you.

STOP (Alliance for Speaking Truth on Prostitution)
1901 Portland Avenue, South
Minneapolis, MN 55404
(612) 872-0684

Chapter Eleven—Throw Down the Sticks and Stones

Books and Curricula

Video—*Molder of Dreams* (church version, 90 minutes, $19.99) or *Teacher of the Year* (secular/school version, 55 minutes, $55.00). Both films are available from Focus on the Family by calling 1-800-232-6459.

Evans, Patricia, *The Verbally Abusive Relationship*. Holbrook, MA: Adams Media Corporation, 1996.

Evans, Patricia. *Verbal Abuse Survivors Speak Out on Relationships and Recovery*. Holbrook, Massachusetts: Adams Media Corporation, 1996.

Bach, George R., and Ronald Deutsch. *Stop! You're Driving Me Crazy!* New York: G. P. Putnam's Sons, 1980.

Bock, Betty. *You Can Make a Difference: Changing Situations That Hurt Others*. Birmingham, AL: Woman's Missionary Union, 1993.

Smith, Malcolm L., *The Peaceful Intervention Program: a Guide Book for Caring for Angry Children and Youth*. Lawrence, KS: Malcolm Smith Consulting, n.d.

Organizations

The National Coalition Against Domestic Violence
P. O. Box 18749
Denver, CO 80218-0749
(303) 839-1852.

Domestic violence section of your local police department.

Chapter Twelve—Put the Sport Back in Sports

Books and Curricula

Sports Spectrum Magazine
P. O. Box 3566
Grand Rapids, MI 49501
1-800-283-8333

Yessick, Tommy, comp. *Sports Ministry for Churches.*
  Nashville: Convention Press, 1996. To order, call 1-800-458-2772. Ask for item #07-673-29.

Organizations

Fellowship of Christian Athletes
8701 Leeds Road
Kansas City, MO 64129
1-800-289-0909

Chapter Thirteen—Control the Television Controls

Organizations

American Family Association
P. O. Drawer 2440
Tupelo, MS 38803
www.afa.net

Preview Family Movie and TV Review
1309 Seminole Drive
Richardson, TX 75080
www.cyserv.com/preview/home.html

TV-Free America and National TV-Turnoff Week
1611 Connecticut Avenue, NW, Suite 3A
Washington, DC 20009
www.essential.org/orgs/tvfa

Books and Curricula

Gore, Tipper. *Raising PG Kids in an X Rated Society.*
  Toronto: Bantam Books, 1987.

Chapter Fourteen—Diffuse Workplace Violence

Marketplace Ministries, Inc.
12900 Preston Road, Suite 1215
Dallas, TX 75230-1328

Chaplaincy Section, North American Mission Board
4200 North Point Parkway
Alpharetta, GA 30022-4176

Chapter Fifteen—Develop a Heart to Help the Poor

Couture, Pamela D. *Blessed Are the Poor? Women's Poverty,*
  Family Policy, and Practical Theology. Nashville: Abingdon
  Press, 1991.

Developmental Resources
You may contact the pastors mentioned in this chapter by
writing to the following addresses:

Rev. Chris McNairy
Westhaven Baptist Church
3415 Millbranch
Memphis, TN 38116

Dr. Dolphus Weary
Mendenhall Ministries
309 Center Street
Mendenhall, MS 39114

Pastor David Kuykendell
Calvary Baptist Church of Oak Cliff
1822 W. 10th Street
Dallas TX 75208

Rev. T. Spencer LeGrand, Sr., Pastor
East Park Baptist Church
12 Ebaugh Avenue
Greenville, SC 29607

Rev. R. B. Cooper
First Baptist Church
515 McCullough
San Antonio, TX 78245

Chapter Sixteen—Promote Mental Wholeness

Bennett, George. *When the Mental Patient Comes Home.*
Philadelphia: Westminster, 1980.

Collins, Gary R. *Christian Counseling: A Comprehensive
Guide.* Dallas: Word Publishing, 1988.

Torrey, E. Fuller. *Surviving Schizophrenia: A Family Manual.*
New York: Perennial Library, 1988.

In your community:
Suicide Prevention Centers
Crisis Intervention Centers
Mental Health Clinics
Hospitals/Hospice Centers
Family Physicians
Clergy

Organizations

American Foundation for Suicide Prevention
120 Wall Street
2nd Floor
New York, NY 10005
(212) 363-3500

A *Directory of Survivor's Groups* is available from:
Suicide Prevention Center, Inc.
P. O. Box 1393
Dayton, OH 45401-1393
(937) 297-4777

Books and Curricula

Bolton, Iris and Curtis Mitchell. *My Son, My Son: A Guide to Healing After a Suicide in the Family.* 2nd ed. Belmore Way, Georgia: Bolton Press, 1983.

Alexander, Victoria. *Words I Never Thought To Speak: Stories of Life in the Wake of Suicide.* New York: Lexington Books, 1991.

Chapter Eighteen—Work Within the Criminal Justice System

Abraham, Henry J. *The Judicial Process: An Introductory Analysis of the Courts in the United States, England, and France.* New York: Oxford University Press, 1975.

Garmire, Bernard L., ed. *Local Government Police Management.* Washington, DC: Institute for Training in Municipal Administration, by the International City Management Association, 1982.

CARING FOR THE CAREGIVER

Why should you consider a ministry to caregivers? "Carry each other's burdens, and in this way you will fulfill the law of Christ" (Gal. 6:2).

Caregivers are among the most overlooked people in American society. Theirs is a role that can be thrust unexpectedly on anyone. Where there is violence, there are victims. Every victim's loved ones and friends find themselves, in the midst of their own shock and grief, serving as caregivers.

While peacemaking is a necessary and worthy goal, as Christians we cannot forge ahead toward that goal and leave the victims of violence unattended in our wake. Those whose lives have been traumatically affected, as well as their caregivers, need our time, attention, and concern.

When we find ourselves in new or uncomfortable situations, we typically rationalize our noninvolvement. But we cannot intentionally or unintentionally turn away from caregivers. We must force ourselves to recognize their need. While we may not be able to empathize completely with their situations, we can make plans to meet their needs.

What is caring for the caregiver? Also referred to as respite care, ministering to a caregiver involves providing support and tangible assistance. The acts of ministry can be onetime, short-term, or ongoing volunteer responsibilities.

Here are some simple guidelines:
• Respect privacy.
• Practice confidentiality.
• Avoid judging, counseling, or offering advice.
• Practice loving-kindness out of sincere motives to demonstrate your caring.

Where do you start? Imagine for a moment that roles are reversed. It is your loved one or friend who has experienced violence firsthand. What could someone do to help carry your burden? Answering that question is an ideal starting point in caring for the caregiver. Next, follow these actions as you begin your ministry to caregivers:
•Identify caregivers in your church and community.
•Ask caregivers what their greatest needs are.
•Recruit volunteers from your church and community.
•Provide training for volunteers.
•Match volunteers with caregivers.

Where should you go from here? One of the most distinctively Christian resources is *hope*. Part of the unique nature of Christian hope lies in its origin. The responsibility for Christian hope is not yours, but God's. You will bring to your caring the conviction that there is One greater than either you or the problem. As a distinctively Christian caregiver, you can become a facilitator of God's hope. Consider these nine practical ways you can become an instrument through which distinctively Christian hope can flow to others.[1]
•Stick with them.
•Be available.
•Reduce anxiety.
•Share the stories of others.
•Accept the other.
•Emphasize the positive.
•Expect failures and limitations.
•Remember that God is with you.
•Be distinctively Christian.

Your caring for a caregiver may simply be the ministry of your presence. Or it may involve your willingness to listen or pray with the caregiver. May you be blessed, as you are being a blessing to a caregiver!

HOW TO DEVELOP A CARE TEAM

Why should you consider beginning a care team? Care teams seek to meet the needs of those with enormous, ongoing needs. The person at the center of the team's attention generally has physical, emotional, financial, and social needs that take their toll on everyone close to him or her, particularly family members. As God's people, He calls us to love and accept others because He first loved and accepted us. As we are obedient in following God, He will lead us through open doors of ministry. The church has historically cared for the sick and injured. Care teams enable several in the church to share the ministry load and lessen the likelihood of individual burnout.

What exactly is a care team? Specifically, a care team is a ministry group consisting of an average of 12 people. Together, the team provides support to the person in need and their loved ones. The care team's assistance is free of charge and may include some of the following actions:
•doing housework
•providing transportation
•offering child care
•cooking
•offering spiritual comfort and support
•identifying helping agencies in the community

People from several congregations can be a care team; or a church may have enough volunteers to form one or more care teams. A team may focus on a specific circumstance such as domestic violence or suicide. If you want to begin a care team, consider following the steps on page 173. Each situation is different. Adapt these guidelines to meet your needs.

Where should we begin? First, educate the entire church. While not every member of your church may be involved in a care team ministry, each can provide prayer support and encouragement to those on care teams. It is also important for the people who receive a care team's ministry to know they are welcomed at the church, and the church needs to be prepared to receive them. Consider the following ideas as you educate your church about the need for a care team:

Conduct a community needs survey. Who are the victims of violence? What services are available to them? Where are the needs for peacemaking in the community? What can the church uniquely do to minister to the community?

Mention the biblical instructions to meet human needs in sermons and special studies.

Hold a communitywide panel discussion with community leaders, social service providers, and those who have first-hand experience in both violence and peacemaking.

Add appropriate resources to the church media library.

Include the violence crisis in prayer.

Invite a person from an existing care team to share what the ministry has meant to him or her and those who have been ministered to.

How will we find volunteers? Announce a meeting for those interested in this ministry. Be sure to mention to volunteers that as part of a team they will not have to do everything themselves. Among others, this ministry calls for the spiritual gifts of service, love, and mercy. Care team members should also demonstrate:

•a compassionate heart.
•an accepting spirit.
•the ability not to judge others.
•the ability to respect confidentiality.
•a willingness to help in whatever way they are needed.

How do we train and prepare? The care team's training should include:
•awareness and education related to the specific need you will address.
•skills in active listening.
•skills in effective communication.
•grief counseling.
•do's and don'ts of ministry.
•how to discuss spiritual issues.

Make team members aware of community resources so they can make referrals when necessary. Help is available for care team training. Check with other churches already doing care team ministry to see how they were trained. Call your Red Cross, crisis centers, a local hospital, or a ministerial association for help and resources for training.

In every phase of training, stress the need for confidentiality. Also emphasize that while care team members may have opportunities to discuss faith, eternal life, and salvation through Jesus Christ, the purpose of a care team is to minister, not proselytize. Any witness given should come naturally and lovingly.

What happens next? Care team ministry makes great demands on emotional and spiritual resources. The congregation can feel a part of the team's ministry by "commissioning" them as ministers of peacemaking on behalf of the congregation. This commissioning may be a special recognition service in which the church affirms the team members and their ministry.

Once you are trained and commissioned, you are ready to find someone to whom you can minister. By networking with crisis centers, hospitals, law enforcement agencies, the local housing authority, social workers, and chaplains, you will discover prospects.

The care team should meet once a month for additional training and supervision. Members can also offer emotional support, raise questions, voice concerns or complaints, give testimonies, and offer practical advice at this time. This meeting is a time for members to share and care for each other.

SUPPORT GROUPS

Why should we consider a support group? Support groups work. Groups sharing a common concern are valuable in enabling healing to begin. People can begin to turn their lives around by working with and attending a support group.

What is a support group? In its simplest definition, a support group is a peer-led group of individuals who share a common need and who meet on a regular basis in confidential settings. They share what is happening in their lives, receive encouragement from each other, and learn and grow in the process.[1]

These basic guidelines are important for support groups:[2]
- The support group must have structure to give it boundaries. Structure also gives members security and calls them to be accountable.
- Support groups must maintain confidentiality, especially in crisis-oriented groups.
- Groups must avoid cross talk (arguing with each other, giving advice, responding with criticism, responding verbally to every statement, confrontations).
- Members must be free to talk or not to talk.
- Facilitators must not process their own issues at the expense of the group.
- Group members must follow the format even if only a few people attend.
- Facilitators and members must be comfortable with silence.
- Group members must follow the group's schedule.
- People who cause problems need to be viewed as people with problems, not problem people.
- Groups must have as their cornerstone the concept of accountability.

•A facilitator needs to recognize personal burnout and take a break, if necessary.
•Facilitators and members must not bring children to meetings.

Where do we start? There is no question that people whose lives have been affected by violence need ministry. Their healing can be a positive step to pave the way to peace in their lives. In your community, what areas of need can you help meet through a support group? Is there someone in your church who feels led to facilitate a group dealing with this common issue?

Support groups can involve the whole church. Every member can provide prayer support and encouragement to those involved with support groups. It is also important for the people who participate in a support group to know they are welcome at the church, and the church needs to be prepared to receive them.

How do we prepare? Identify the group's facilitator, as well as people and resources that can provide training for the facilitator. Then, create an environment in which people can grow. Consider these factors which influence growth: regularly scheduled meetings with a length of one-and-a-half to two hours; groups in which members decide how many sessions they will have (generally 6 to 12 sessions); and a size of 8 to 20 persons, in addition to the facilitator(s). Also provide a meeting place that is private and comfortable. Give the group a positive name to allay possible fears of those who may need or want to join it.

How do we find someone to whom we can minister? Publicize the group. Network with crisis centers, hospitals, law enforcement agencies, the local housing authority, social workers, or chaplains. Let them know when and where your group will be held. Ask them to refer those they think will benefit from the group.

Where do we go from here? Evaluate the effectiveness of the group. Is it meeting needs? Are people experiencing healing? Consider ways to enhance or expand your support group ministry.

MENTORING

Why should I become a mentor? One of the greatest gifts you can give another person is to invest yourself in his or her growth and development. People who have been victims of violence can often benefit from a mentoring relationship. Such a positive relationship built on trust and mutuality can lift someone from a dangerous lifestyle, enable healing to begin, or lead to life-changing empowerment.

What is mentoring? Mentoring is sharing the sense of God's impact in your life journey; making an emotional, spiritual, and physical deposit of seeds into someone's life to impact their *season* of life.[1] The Ten Commandments of Mentoring are:[2]

•Establish the mentoring.
•Jointly agree on the purpose of the relationship.
•Determine the regularity of interaction.
•Determine the type of accountability.
•Set up communication mechanisms.
•Clarify the level of confidentiality.
•Set the life cycle of the relationship.
•Evaluate the relationship from time to time.
•Modify expectations to fit the real-life mentoring situation.
•Bring closure to the mentoring relationship.

Where do I start?
•Begin with prayer.
•Continue where there is a desire.
•Identify where there is a need. Locate one whose life has been impacted by violence. Be intentional about establishing a mentoring relationship.

How do I prepare? Grow in your understanding of mentoring by reading about this special relationship. Seek guidance from crisis centers, chaplains, or professional counselors. Participate in recommended training. Do not hesitate to ask others to keep you and the person you mentor in their prayers.

Where do I go from here? Recognize your mentoring relationship as a ministry. Respect commitments you make to the one you mentor as a commitment to God. Expect joy as well as bumps along the journey. When it is complete, remember to celebrate God at work in both of you!

NETWORKING

Why should we consider networking? Ralph Neighbor has identified the seven last words of the church as "we never did it that way before." When it comes to networking with other helping agencies in the Christian community, often we have not done it at all! In order for your peacemaking efforts to be most effective, you cannot carry them out in a vacuum.

What is networking? Technology would lead us to understand networking in computer terms. If our computers are equipped with the right hardware and have adequate software support, it is possible for us to "network." Sharing files and electronically communicating with each other is characteristic of networking that can take place between churches and helping agencies. The goal of networking is to avoid duplication of efforts, to share information, to communicate, and to enhance the efforts of all involved.

Where do we start?

Determine the area(s) of peacemaking that you, your group, or your church want to enhance.

Identify social service and helping agencies in your community. What programs, projects, resources, or services do they provide? Are there ways you can work together on common goals?

Locate other churches or civic organizations in the community with common interests and goals. Are there ways you can work together?

Identify the resources available to you. Don't forget that facilities and volunteers are as important as financial resources.

179

What's next? In order for networking to be effective, it must be intentional. Is there someone who can be the liaison from your church or group to others with whom you are working? It is vital to keep communication channels open, and that can be more easily facilitated if someone has that responsibility. Networking is a relationship of mutuality. Each entity involved in the project or service will benefit from cooperation and support.

PEACEMAKING PROJECT PLAN

Why should we have a peacemaking project? With worldwide media coverage available to almost everyone, it is virtually impossible to escape information on the prevalence of violence in our communities today. Many times, all the motivation Christians need to work toward ending violence is the opportunity to serve. Your peacemaking project is an opportunity to serve as well as being a specific action toward curbing violence.

Why plan? The old adage is true whether we like to admit it or not: To fail to plan is to plan to fail. Your project plans are road maps to develop, implement, and evaluate your project toward paving the way to peace in your community. Consider these guidelines:

- Select a project suggested in this book or design one of your own.
- Match needs with resources to complete the project.
- Determine objectives.
- Commit to the project.
- Communicate your plans.
- Recruit and train needed volunteers.
- Gather needed materials or resources.
- Conduct the project.
- Evaluate the project.
- Tell others what you accomplished.

Project Planning Sheet

Project:

Desired outcome of the project:

Date: Time: Place:

Target issue or group:

Contact person: Address: Phone:

Other group participating in the project:

Contact person: Address: Phone:

Other group participating in the project:

Contact person: Address: Phone:

Other group participating in the project:

Contact person: Address: Phone:

Training needed by participants:

How training will be received:

Planning and work to be done in advance:

Due date: Person responsible/phone number:

Supplies needed:

Due date: Person responsible/phone number:

Actions to be done during project:

Due dates: Persons responsible/phone numbers:

Witnessing opportunities anticipated:

Transportation needed:

Budget expenditures:

Evaluation date: Evaluation guidelines:

APPENDIX G

SCREENING VOLUNTEERS

Why is screening important? Churches have unique features that can make them susceptible to incidents of child molestation. Churches tend to be trusting and unsuspecting institutions. Some churches do nothing to screen volunteer workers. Churches provide ample opportunities for unsupervised close personal contact between adults and children. Child molesters are attracted to institutions in which they have immediate access to potential victims in an atmosphere of complete trust—the church. And most churches struggle to get adequate help for children and youth programs, so willing volunteers are welcomed.[1]

Where do I begin? Every church needs to establish policies and procedures for volunteer selection, supervision, obligation to report specific behaviors, and response to allegations.

To protect the children and youth of the church and community and to legally protect the church, each church needs to adequately screen all paid and volunteer workers.

PRIMARY SCREENING PROCEDURES

This provides the church with the best potential to reduce legal risk. This procedure consists of the following components:[2]
•an employment application.
•a screening form.
•a personal interview.
•reference checks.
•completion of a criminal records check authorization form—to be used when considered appropriate.

183

PRACTICAL SCREENING TIPS

Churches should keep the following considerations in mind when implementing a screening procedure:[3]
•Confirm identity.
•Screen all workers.
•Lower risk.
•Use professional help.
•Examine sample forms.
•Fulfill legal requirements.
•Maintain confidentiality.

CRIMINAL RECORDS CHECK

Criminal records checks ordinarily should be viewed as a procedure that may be desirable if questions are raised about a particular applicant or worker.[4]

There are different types of criminal records checks. The most common are name checks and fingerprint checks. The fee for the check varies. To determine what information you can obtain from the check and the fee, ask your local law enforcement agency.

Is screening too burdensome? If the use of screening procedures and reference forms seems overly burdensome, consider the following:[5]

One insurance company executive has described as an epidemic the number of church lawsuits as a result of sexual molestation.

Your church liability insurance policy may exclude or limit coverage for acts of child molestation.

The screening procedure is designed primarily to provide a safe and secure environment for the children and youth of your church.

The relatively minor inconvenience involved in establishing a screening procedure is a small price to pay for protecting the church from the negative consequences that often accompany an incident of molestation.

In some cases, church board members may be personally liable for acts of child molestation.

Is screening important? To answer that question, ask any child, youth, parent, or member whose church has been involved in a sexual abuse incident.

TEACHING PLAN

Objective: Determine the desired outcome of your conference. Consider this sample objective: As a result of this conference, participants will gain a basic understanding of any one topic you choose in this book, and explore ways of being peacemakers.

Length: This plan will allow you to plan for a one- to one-and-one-half-hour conference. You can lengthen the conference by inviting a guest speaker to participate, expanding the Bible study, or showing an appropriate video.

Audience: Who will attend your conference? Keep your audience in mind as you make your plans.

Preparation:
•Familiarize yourself with this teaching plan.
•Read (or reread) the chapter of this book you have selected or have been asked to teach.
•Study the Biblical Foundations referenced in the chapter.
•Identify any helping agency, crisis center, or individual in your community that may be familiar with your topic. Plan to interview a representative or arrange for someone to speak during your conference.
•Preview any related video to determine the appropriateness of the content for your conference.
•Collect any resources you will need during the conference.
•Prepare any handouts or visuals.

Note to the conference leader: This conference outline is provided as a guide. You do not need to follow it exactly. Use information from your reading of this book and other materials as well as personal experiences as conference content. Help your conferees as best you can to be prepared to pave the way to peace!

LEADING THE CONFERENCE:

Early Arrivers Activity: Supply a name tag for each participant. Ask each person to write his or her name on one side of the tag and one idea for peacemaking on the other side.

Introductory Activity: Ask participants to form groups of four. Ask them within their groups to share their names and ideas for peacemaking. After about five minutes, call participants together. Briefly overview the conference.

Biblical Foundations: Read or ask some in advance to read the biblical passages referenced in the chapter you have chosen to teach. If the objective of your conference is an overview of peacemaking, you may choose "Blessed are the peacemakers" (Matt. 5:9) as the biblical basis for your conference. Present (or ask someone in advance to prepare) a brief study of the Scripture.

Overview: Prepare and present a brief overview of the area of violence your conference is addressing. How widespread is the problem? Who are the victims? What is the cause? Is the problem increasing?

Reality check: Provide participants with pages from current newspapers or newsmagazines. Divide them into groups, or allow them to work alone. Ask half of the groups or individuals to locate and count the number of stories, editorials, obituaries, and/or cartoons that are linked to violence. How many are related to the topic you are dealing with? Ask the other group or individuals to locate and count references to peacemaking or positive actions taken to address violence. Ask several participants to report their findings.

Ask: *Did you discover a trend?* Point out that violence is common. Violence is an everyday fact. It occurs in all kinds of places and to all kinds of people. Yet, the identifiable efforts to curb violence are less visible, if not less numerous.

The church has been concerned about violence for 2,000 years. Today many Christians are concerned about its prevalence. However, being concerned is not enough. It is time for Christians to become peacemakers. Together we can pave the way to peace.

What's working: From the chapter you are teaching, share stories, ministry models, and ministry/peacemaking ideas. Also ask participants to share related ideas and stories.

Ready, set, act: Lead learners to name specific actions your group, church, or community can take to pave the way to peace. List their suggestions on a chalkboard, a large piece of paper, or a projected overhead cel. Then review the list. Which ones are feasible for your church or group to undertake? At this point in the conference, you may choose to ask for a commitment from conferees willing to plan this effort. You may also ask participants to return to their groups and assign them all or portions of the project planning sheet (see p. 182) to complete.

Conclusion: Compile a completed project planning sheet. Ask for volunteers to present the plan to the appropriate church leaders. Close with prayer.

PROJECT LITERACY

No single solution can end violence. But what if there were one accessible, fairly inexpensive, proven method to deter persons from beginning a violent lifestyle? There is! Statistically, a literate person is less likely to be involved in violent behaviors than one who cannot read.

Mobilizing available resources to pave the way to peace through increasing literacy will create a safer world. Literacy, as defined by the National Literacy Act of 1991, is "an individual's ability to read, write, and speak in English and compute and solve problems at levels of proficiency necessary to function on the job and in society, to achieve one's goals, and develop one's knowledge and potential." One in five US citizens is functionally illiterate.

Here are some practical ways to help stop illiteracy in our nation:
•Observe National Literacy Day.
•Participate in National Literacy Sunday.
•Learn to recognize literacy needs and make referrals to persons and programs that can help.
•Volunteer to teach someone to read.
•Host and/or participate in an adult reading and writing workshop.
•Adopt a local school and participate in the Time Warner "Time to Read" national program or provide classroom tutors.
•Become a literacy advocate in your community or state.

For more information on adult reading and writing, contact your State Department of Education's Adult Education Section, your local Literacy Council, or the Church and Community Ministries Unit of the North American Mission Board.

ENDNOTES

Chapter Two—Practicing Peace in Communities

[1]Robert Famighetti, ed. *The World Almanac® and Book of Facts*, (Mahweh, NJ: World Almanac Books, 1997), 958.

[2]Carol Marbin Miller "Tampa boy, 2, dies after beating," *St. Petersburg Times*. October 29, 1997. Web site address: sptimes.com/News2/102997/NATIONAL/Tampa_boy_dies.html.

[3]National Child Abuse and Neglect Clearinghouse Statistics Desk. Web site address: www.calib.com/nccanch/services/stats.htm.

[4]"Teen Who Put Baby in Bag Gets Jail Time." *The [Philadelphia] Inquirer*, October 24 1997. Web site address: www.phillynews.com/inquirer/97/Oct/24/city/CBABY24.htm.

[5]Harry Burbach and the Curry School of Education. *Violence and the Public Schools*. Web site address: aace.virginia.edu/~rkb3b/Hal/SchoolViolence.html.

[6]"DA: Ran Crack Biz in East Harlem." *Philadelphia Daily News*, October 30 1997. Web site address: www.phillynews.com/daily_news/97/Oct/30/national/GANG30.htm.

[7]Federal Gang Violence Act of 1997. Web site by Senator Dianne Feinstein based on the Federal Gang Violence Act of 1997. Address: www.senate.gov/member/ca/feinstein/general/gangs.html.

[8]"Gang Facts," ©1996 by Library Publications, 2805 Alvarado Lane, Plymouth, MN 55447. Web site address: www.winternet.com/~publish/gangfact.htm.

[9]Bill Wallace, "San Francisco Man Held Under New Law. Domestic Violence Act Means Federal Charges," October 24 1997. *San Francisco Chronicle*, Web site address: www.sfgate.com/cgi-bin/chronicle/article.cgi/file=MN46609.DTL&directory=/chronicle/archive/1997/10/24

[10]"Women Usually Victimized by Offenders They Know," US Department of Justice, Bureau of Justice Statistics, (August 16 1995). Web site address: www.ojp.usdoj.gov/pub/bjs/press/femvied.pr.

[11]Leef Smith, "Man Convicted in Attack Using Date-Rape Pill." *Washington Post*, October 24 1997. Web site address: washingtonpost.com/wp-srv/WPlate/1997-10/24/1551-102497-idx.html.

[12]"Rape Statistics," taken from an April 23, 1992, report from the National Victim Center, Web site address: www.cs.utk.edu/~bartley/sa/stats.html.

[13]"According to Housing and Urban Development estimates, Seven Million People Experienced Homelessness . . .," *The Stanford Daily Online*, vol. 208 (January 23 1996). Web site address: daily.stanford.org/1-23-96/OPINIONS/OPSTUES23C.html.

[14]US Census Bureau, "Poverty: 1996 Highlights." Web site address: www.census.gov/hhes/poverty/poverty96/pov96hi.html.

[15]Statistics from the National Aging Resource Center on Elder Abuse, 1990, as quoted under "Elder Abuse" at the Web site www.cybergrrl.com/planet/dv//stat/statgen.html.

[16]John Wildermuth. "Racial Incidents Rock Carlmont High School." *San Francisco Chronicle*, October 28 1997, A13. Web site address: www.sfgate.com/cgi-bin/chronicle/article.cgi?file=MN43040.DTL&directory=/chronicle/archive/1997/10/28.

[17]US Department of Justice, Criminal Justice Information Services (CJIS) Division, "Hate Crime-1995." Web site address: www.fbi.gov/ucr/hatecm.htm.

[18]"Violence in the Workplace." Web site address: ftp.cdc.gov/niosh/violabst.html.

[19]D. Enfield Berry, "Targeting Verbal Abuse." Web site address: www.pathcom.com/~moron/artists/first.htm.

[20]National Center for Injury Prevention and Control, "Suicide in the United States." Web site address: www.cdc.gov/ncipc/dvp/suifacts.htm.

[21]"Air Force Concludes A-10 Pilot Was Suicide in Colorado Crash," *The Washington Post*, October 25, 1997. Web site address: washingtonpost.com/wp-srv/WPlate/1997-10/25/0831-102597-idx.html.

[22]"Suicide in the United States."

[23]APA (American Psychiatric Association) Online, "Violence and Mental Illness." Web site address: www.psych.org/public_info/VIOLEN~1.HTM

[24]"Judge Find Nuns' Attacker Not Responsible Because of Mental Illness," October 16, 1996. ©1996 The Associated Press. Web site address: www2.nando.net/newsroom/ntn/nation/101696/nation4_22781.html.

[25]Barbara Laker, "More Kids Going to Prison," *Philadelphia Daily News.* October 28, 1997. Web site address: www.phillynew.com/daily_news/97/Oct/28/local/JJUD28.htm.

[26]Bureau of Justice Statistics of the US Department of Justice, "Key Crime and Justice Facts at a Glance." Web site address: www.ojp.usdoj.gov/bjs/glance.htm.

[27]American Medical Association release, "Advocacy & Communications," © 1995–1997 American Medical Association. Web site address: www.ama-assn.org/ad-com/releases/1996/mv0909.htm.

[28]Neilson Media Research 1993 statistic, as quoted in "Facts About Media Violence." by the American Medical Association. Web site address: www.ama-assn.org/ad-com/releases/1996/mvfacts.htm.

[29]Center for Media and Public Affairs 1994 statistic, as quoted in "Facts About Media Violence," by the American Medical Association. Web site address: www.ama-assn.org/ad-com/releases/1996/mvfacts.htm.

Chapter Four—Care for, Love, and Protect Children

[1]Jeffery W. Scott, *Does Your Child's World Scare You? Making the World a Better Place for Children.* (Macon, GA: Peake Road, 1997), 43.

[2]Ibid., 44.

[3]Mary Pipher, PhD, *The Shelter of Each Other* (New York: G.P. Putnam's Sons, 1996), 92.

[4]Scott, *Does Your Child's World Scare You?,* 41.

[5]Hillary Rodham Clinton, *It Takes A Village And Other Lessons Children Teach Us.* (New York: Touchstone, 1996): 276.

[6]"Study Says More Children Being Abused," *The (Louisville, Kentucky) Courier-Journal,* September 19, 1996, A3.

[7]Ibid.

[8]US Department of Justice, Federal Bureau of Investigation, Uniform Crime Reports, "Crime in the United States: 1994," November 19, 1995.

[9]Children's Defense Fund press release, April 9, 1996, 2.

[10]"10 Myths and Realities," *Children's Defense Fund Reports* 17, no. 2 (January 1996): 9.

[11]Doris Harris, "Preschool Partners: Birmingham, AL," *The Journal of Family Ministry* 10, no. 3 (winter 1996): 34–36.

[12]Children's Defense Fund brochure, "Stand for Children Every Day."

[13]Jeffery W. Scott, *Does Your Child's World Scare You?*, 52.

[14]"A Safe Place for Kids," *Salt of the Earth* 17, no 1 (January/February 1997): 7.

Chapter Five—Nurture and Equip Youth

[1]William DeJong, PhD, *Preventing Interpersonal Violence Among Youth* (Department of Health and Social Behavior, Harvard School of Public Health, November 1994): 2.

[2]Dick Schaaf, "Playgrounds or Battlegrounds? Violence in School Is a Piece of a Much Bigger Puzzle," *Friendly Exchange* (summer 1995): 24–25.

[3]Ted Gest and Victoria Pope, "Crime Time Bomb," *U.S. News and World Report*, March 25, 1996, 30.

[4]Ibid., 36.

[5]American Psychological Association, "Violence and Youth: Psychology's Response," vol. 1, *Summary Report of the American Psychological Association Commission on Violence and Youth*, 12.

[6] Ibid., 12–13.

[7] Deborah Prothrow-Stith, MD, *Deadly Consequences: How Violence is Destoying Our Teenage Population and a Plan to Begin Solving the Problem.* (New York: HarperCollins Publishers, 1991), 20.

[8] Randy Arndt, "School Violence on Rise, Survey Says: Not Just a Big City Issue," *Nation's Cities Weekly (Washington, DC)* 17, no. 45, (November 7 1994), 1f.

[9] Mark Sanders, *Preventing Gang Violence in Your School*, (Minneapolis: Johnson Institute, 1995), 1.

[10] Richard Weissbourd, *The Vulnerable Child: What Really Hurts America's Children and What We Can Do About It*, (Reading, MA: Addison-Wesley Publishing Co., 1996), 113.

[11] American Psychological Association, "Violence and Youth," 28.

[12] Ibid., 19.

[13] Weissbourd, *The Vulnerable Child*, 115.

[14] Cathy Spatz Widom, "The Cycle of Violence" (Washington, DC: National Institute of Justice, October 1992), 5.

[15] Strasburger, Victor C. *Adolescents and the Media: Medical and Psychological Impact*. Vol. 33 of *Developmental Clinical Psychology and Psychiatry*. (Thousand Oak, CA: Sage Publications, 1995), 19.

Chapter Six—Diminish the Lure of Gangs

[1] Sylvester Monroe, "Life in the 'Hood." *Time*, June 15, 1992, 38.

[2] Barbara Backer, "Coming Soon to a Suburb Near You," *Woman's Day*, April 5, 1994, 23.

Chapter Seven—Cultivate Domestic Harmony

[1] Erin Hanafy, "Witness Beyond Death," *Waco Tribune-Herald*, (March 28 1997), 1C, 3C.

[2] Liza N. Burby, *Family Violence*, (San Diego, CA: Lucent Books, Inc. 1996), 17.

[3] Bureau of Justice Statistics, "Women Usually Victimzed by Offenders They Know," (US Department of Justice), August 16 1995.

[4] Joyce Price, "Report Is a Reminder That Men Are Battered Too," *The Washington Times*, January 31, 1994, sec. A.

[5] Burby, *Family Violence*, 17.

Chapter Eight—Respect Your Elders

[1] Joseph P. Shapiro, "The Elderly's Vulnerability to Abuse Is Exaggerated," in *Family Violence*, ed. A. E. Sadler, (San Diego, CA: Greenhaven Press, 1996), 139.

[2]Ibid.

[3]Ibid.

[4]Marjorie Valbrum, "As America Ages, Abuse Grows Old," *Philadelphia Inquirer.* February 6, 1994, A1f.

[5]Michael Dorgan, "Elder Abuse: The Crime of the '90s," *San Jose Mercury News.* May 23, 1993, 1Af.

[6]Ibid.

[7]Frank Stagg, *The Bible Speaks on Aging,* (Nashville: Broadman Press, 1981), 179.

Chapter Nine—Build Bridges of Love

[1]Robert Famighetti, ed., *The World Almanac® and Book of Facts,* (Mahweh, NJ: World Almanac Books, 1997), 378–79.

[2]Bureau of Justice Statistics of the US Department of Justice, "Hate Crime—1995." Web site address: www.fbi.gov/ucr/hatecm/htm.

[3]Bureau of Justice Statistics of the US Department of Justice, "National Crime Victimization Survey," December 1994. Web site address: www.ncjrs.org/txtfiles/ybmv.txt.

[4]According to a 1995 study by the Bureau of Justice Statistics, "Victim Characteristics." Web site address: www.ojp.usdoj.gov/bjs/cvict_v.htm.

[5]Canadian Anti-racism Education and Research (CAERS), "How to Deal with Racial Violence." Web site address: www.antiracist.com/resource/hate-broc.html.

Chapter Ten—The Unspeakable Crime

[1]The American Medical Association, "Sexual Assault: The Silent Violent Epidemic." Quoted in Otto Johnson, ed., *Information Please Almanac ® Atlas & Yearbook, 1997,* 50th ed. (Boston: Houghton Mifflin Co., 1997), 430.

[2]Ibid.

[3]Cynthia Kubetin and James Mallory, *Shelter from the Storm: Hope for Survivors of Sexual Abuse* (Nashville: Lifeway Press, 1995).

[4]Ibid., 31–36.

Chapter Eleven—Throw Down the Sticks and Stones

[1] W.I.S.E. (Women's Issues and Social Empowerment), "Domestic Violence Information Manual." Web site address: www.infoxchange.net.au/wise/DVAbuse.htm.

[2] *Family Violence Profession Education Task Force* (1991), 63, quoted on W.I.S.E. Web site.

[3] Patricia Evans, *The Verbally Abusive Relationship,* (Holbrook, MA: Adams Media Corporation, 1996), 25.

[4] George R. Bach and Ronald Deutsch, *Stop! You're Driving Me Crazy* (New York: G. P. Putnam's Sons, 1980), 272–73, quoted in Evans, *The Verbally Abusive Relationship*, 25–26.

[5] Evans, *The Verbally Abusive Relationship*, 51.

[6] Ibid., 50.

[7] Ibid., 81–85.

[8] Ibid., 125–28.

[9] Yvonne M. Vissing, et al., "Summary of Verbal Aggression by Parents and Psychosocial Problems of Children," *Child Abuse and Neglect*, vol. 15 (1991), 223–39. Web site address: www. infoxchange.net.au/wise/DV-Abuse. htm.

[10] Marilyn Elias, "Siblings' Verbal Abuse Has Lasting Effects," *USA Today*, September 9, 1997. Web site address: www.usatoday.com/life/health/family/violence/lhfvi004.htm.

[11] Evans, *The Verbally Abusive Relationship*, 41–42.

[12] Ibid., 29.

[13] Lawrence O. Richards, *Expository Dictionary of Bible Words* (Grand Rapids, MI: Regency Reference Library, 1985), 633.

[14] Ibid., 634–636.

[15] Robert Fulghum, *All I Really Need to Know I Learned in Kindergarten: Uncommon Thoughts on Common Things* (New York: Random House, Inc., 1989), 14; quoted in Evans, *The Verbally Abusive Relationship*, 23.

Chapter Thirteen—Control the Television Controls

[1]Mediascope National Television Violence Study, February 1996.
To order a copy of the study, contact:
Mediascope, Inc.
12711 Ventura Boulevard, Suite 280
Studio City, CA 91604

[2]*Telecommunications Act of 1996.* US Public Law 104–104, 104th Cong., sec.
551, February 8, 1996.

[3]For more information, contact:
TV-Free America
1611 Connecticut Avenue NW, Suite 3A
Washington, DC 20009
Phone: (202) 887-0436
Fax: (202) 518-5560
tvfa@essential.org

Chapter Fifteen—Develop a Heart to Help the Poor

[1]Statistics provided by Dr. Gary Farley, Town and Country Director (North
American Mission Board).

[2]David Claerbaut, *Urban Ministry* (Grand Rapids, MI: Zondervan Publishing
House, 1983), 69.

[3]Robert Morris, *Encyclopedia of Social Work* (New York: National Association
of Social Workers, 1971), 901.

[4]Anthony T. Evans, *America's Only Hope* (Chicago: Moody Press, 1990),
12–13.

[5]Ibid., 13.

[6]Kay Coles James, *Transforming American from the Inside Out.* (Grand Rapids,
MI: Zondervan Publishing House, 1995), 140–41.

[7]Evans, *America's Only Hope*, 13.

[8]Ronald J. Sider, *Rich Christians In an Age of Hunger: A Biblical Study* (Downers Grove, IL: Intervarsity Press, 1997), 68–69.

Chapter Sixteen—Promote Mental Wholeness

[1]Gary R. Collins, *Christian Counseling: A Comprehensive Guide*, rev. ed. (Dallas: Word Publishing, 1988), 470.

[2]Ibid., 473.

[3]Ibid., 469–70.

Chapter Seventeen—Lessen the Likelihood of Suicide

[1]National Center for Injury Prevention and Control. Web site address: www.cdc.gov/ncipc/dvp/suifacts.htm

[2]Rita Robinson, *Survivors of Suicide* (Santa Monica, CA: IBS Press, 1989), 93–115.

[3]For more information, contact Judie Smith, Crisis Specialist for Dallas Public Schools, Psychological and Diagnostic Services, 12532 Nuestra Drive, Dallas, TX 75230.

[4]Dave Capuzzi, *Suicide Prevention in the Schools* (Alexandria, VA: American Counseling Association, 1994), 102–103.

[5]Ibid., 92.

[6]Robinson, *Survivors of Suicide*, xiii.

Chapter Eighteen—Work Within the Criminal Justice System

[1]Bernard L. Garmire, ed., *Local Government Police Management* (Washington, DC: Institute for Training in Municipal Administration by the International City Management Assoc., 1982), 19.

[2]Quoted in Henry J. Abraham, *The Judicial Process: An Introductory Analysis of the Courts in the United States, England, and France* (New York: Oxford University Press, 1975), 3.

[3]Garmire, *Local Government Police Management*, 5.

[4]Ibid., 13.

[5]Norval Morris, *The Future of Imprisonment* (Chicago: The University of Chicago Press, 1974), x.

[6]*Violent Crime in America: Recommendations of the IACP Summit on Violent Crime*, report from the International Association of Chiefs of Police Crime Summit, April 27, 1993, sec. 1.

[7]Garmire, *Local Government Police Management*, 15.

Appendix A—Caring for the Caregiver

[1]Kenneth C. Haugk, *Christian Caregiving: A Way of Life* (Minneapolis: Augsburg Publishing House, 1984), 147–54.

Appendix C—Support Groups

[1]Sara Hines Martin, *Meeting Needs Through Support Groups* (Birmingham: New Hope, 1992), 12.

[2]Ibid., 20–22.

Appendix D—Mentoring

[1]Esther Burroughs, *A Garden Path to Mentoring* (Birmingham: New Hope, 1997), 7.

[2]Paul D. Stanley, and J. Robert Clinton, *Connecting* (Colorado Springs: Navpress, 1992), 197–98.

Appendix G—Screening Volunteers

[1]Richard R. Hammar, Steven W. Klipowicz, and James F. Cobble, Jr., *Reducing the Risk of Child Sexual Abuse in Your Church*, Church Law and Tax Report (Matthews, NC: Christian Ministry Resources, 1993), 19.

[2]Ibid, 30–33.

[3]Ibid, 34.

[4]Ibid, 40.

[5]Ibid, 42–43.